INSTRUCTOR'S MANUAL AND TEST BANK

to accompany

SENTENCE DYNAMICS
AN ENGLISH SKILLS WORKBOOK
Sixth Edition

Constance Immel

West Los Angeles College, Emeritus

Florence Sacks

West Lost Angeles College, Emeritus

PEARSON
Longman

New York Boston San Francisco
London Toronto Sydney Tokyo Singapore Madrid
Mexico City Munich Paris Cape Town Hong Kong Montreal

Instructor's Manual and Test Bank to accompany Immel/Sacks, *Sentence Dynamics: An English Skills Workbook, Sixth Edition*

Copyright ©2005 Pearson Education, Inc.

ISBN: 0-321-14561-5

1 2 3 4 5 6 7 8 9 10—OPM—07 06 05

TABLE OF CONTENTS

PREFACE

The sixth edition of *Sentence Dynamics* has been revised and updated. So, too, has the *Instructor's Manual,* which includes the following:

- Answers for all Text Exercises, Group Activities, Editing Practices, and Practice Tests
- Tests for Chapters 1 through 9, Forms A, B, and C
- A Midterm Exam
- A Final Exam
- Answers for all Chapter Tests and Midterm and Final Exams

No matter what your present teaching methods may be, *Sentence Dynamics, Sixth Edition*, can be adapted to meet the requirements of most developmental writing courses. The following describes the techniques we use in our classes that you may find helpful. During the first week of the semester, we explain the ways students can use the *Sentence Dynamics* workbook to their greatest advantage. We introduce the last chapter, "Writing a Paragraph," during the first or second meeting of class and assign the exercises in it at regular intervals throughout the semester. We ask them to write their answers in the book in pencil so they can correct their work easily and neatly. We urge our students to develop the habit of consulting a dictionary routinely and to regard it as their first resource when they have a question about the work in their books.

Our students complete the exercises in the chapter and the summary before attempting the Practice Test. We collect and review the Practice Test with the students before they take the Chapter Test. We encourage them to use a dictionary during the test, but they may not consult their workbooks.

We have provided three forms of each Chapter Test to enable you to vary the questions if you teach multiple sections of the same course using the workbook. To further prevent sharing of test questions, we collect and file all tests after reviewing the answers with the students. Although some teachers have requested Scantron-scored tests we have avoided the machine-scored test format and we have formulated the questions on the grammar tests so that they resemble the problems students sometimes have when they are writing papers.

To develop the students' writing skills, we use *Sentence Dynamics, Sixth Edition*, in conjunction with weekly writing assignments and the Sentence Combining Lessons. The writing assignments are designed to help the students develop content and a sense of organization in their writing. We have added new exercises encouraging group participation in the development of writing assignments and the discussion of completed papers among peer groups. Doing exercises in a workbook can never substitute for the experience of applying the skills learned each week through writing and proofreading. Therefore, as the students are progressing through *Sentence Dynamics*, they are also applying the principles learned in it to writing assignments.

We assign a minimum of one writing assignment a week, alternating between in-class and out-of-class assignments. At the end of the course, students who have completed nine Chapter Tests, a Midterm Exam, and a minimum of 14 writing assignments take a Final Exam and complete a final writing assignment.

These classroom techniques have developed out of our experience with teaching students who have had limited success in English classes before entering college. In our program, we encourage the students to share with the instructor the responsibility for improving their writing skills.

Constance Immel

Florence Sacks

ANSWER KEY TO TEXT EXERCISES

Chapter 1

Exercise 1A
They, performer, Everyone, artists, people, man, experts, man, Jugglers

Exercise 2A Answers will vary.

Exercise 2B

   X   N   N X   N   X   N
1. on, highway 2. Rain, last 3. drivers, cautious 4. surface,
N   N   N   N   X   N   X   N
road 5. Buick, brakes 6. John, tried 7. foot, off 8. car,
X   N   N   X   X
across 9. fender, bumper 10. Both, away

Exercise 2C Answers will vary.

Exercise 3A Answers will vary.

Exercise 3B
1. dogs 2. dates 3. tricks 4. tests 5. sales

Exercise 3C
1. skies 2. days 3. ladies 4. turkeys 5. counties 6-10: answers will vary

Exercise 3D
1. brushes 2. watches 3. buses 4. waltzes 5. taxes 6-10: answers will vary

Exercise 3E
1. beliefs 2. halves 3. hooves or hoofs 4. shelves 5. wives

Exercise 3F
1. sopranos 2. vetoes 3. tomatoes 4. tornadoes (tornados) 5. pianos

Exercise 3G
1. mice 2. teeth 3. women 4. children 5. men

Exercise 3H Answers will vary.

Exercise 3I
1. tutors 2. students, plugs 3. students, pages 4. students 5. minutes
6. tutors 7. instructors, outlets 8. tutors, students 9. students 10. instructors

Review of Plurals

1. boys	shoes
2. shelves	dishes
3. supplies	countries

4. models	bikinis
5. addresses	churches
6. applicants	tests
7. keys	books
8. boxes	photos
9. tomatoes	
10. secretaries	duties

Exercise 4A
1. the cats' names 2. their owners' commands 3. Christy's bed
4. Christy's mother 5. Ginny's food

Exercise 4B Sentences will vary.
1. ladies' shoes 2. Juan's new car 3. comedian's jokes 4. bird's
wing 5. heroes' medals

Exercise 4C
1. New York City's its 2. his city's 3. Today's America's 4. salt's our
5. engineer's people's 6. drivers' their 7. politicians' his 8. engineer's
9. New York City's engineer's 10. Their their New York's their

Editing Practice
1. women's 2. company's 3. year's 4. weeks' 5. months' 6. store's
7. employer's or employers'

Exercise 4D
1. Saturday's 2. week's 3. country's 4. month's 5. plane's

Exercise 4E
1. students' 2. no apostrophe 3. customer's or customers' 4. parents' 5. no apostrophe

Exercise 4F
1. traveler's 2. passengers' 3. visitors' 4. aide's 5. volunteers' 6. worker's 7. tourist's 8. family's
9. motorists' 10. Doris's

Exercise 4G
1. daughter's 2. Larry's 3. Honda's 4. Larry's 5. agent's 6. day's
7. weeks' 8. Larry's

Exercise 4H
1. Lori, junior, Central College, students, summer 2. spring, listings,
newspaper, qualifications 3. companies, applicant, weeks 4. Choice,
company, bookkeeper 5. impression, dress, earrings 6. manager,
background, experience 7. end, interview, Lori, offer, job, weeks

Group Activity
1. month's 2. kangaroo's 3. Mr. Atlas's 4. people's 5. twins' 6. dawn's
7. brother-in-law's 8. sopranos' 9. Timothy and Kelly's 10. Martinez's

Editing Practice
1. Change you to I 2. Change you to they 3. Change you to they 4. Change you to I and your to my

Exercise 5A
1. You're 2. They're 3. Who's 4. It's 5. They're 6. hers 7. theirs 8. its, your 9. Whose 10. You're

Exercise 6A Sentences will vary.

Lesson 7 Suggested Sentences
A. Scott carefully read the detailed, complicated instructions. B. A powerful windstorm knocked down several trees in our neighborhood last night. C. Sumi rescued a nine-year-old boy from drowning last summer at Camp Arrowhead. D. The tall woman wore a red-striped blouse and a black cotton skirt. E. I have always wanted to be an athlete like Jackie Robinson or Reggie Jackson and make a million dollars.

Chapter Summary
1. common nouns 2. proper nouns 3. possessive 4. number, gender

Practice Test
I. 1. noun
2. other
3. other
4. noun
5. other
6. other
7. noun
8. other
9. noun
10. noun

II. 1. Mrs. Tracy ticket Kansas City
2. nurse appointments day
3. end innings run
4. class students library
5. poodle water sunbathers

III. 1. weeks week's
2. Terrys Terry's
3. coachs coach's
4. drivers driver's
5. audiences audience's

IV. 1. debaters'
2. senators'
3. children's
4. consumers' or consumer's
5. puppies'

V. 1. <u>you</u> she
2. <u>they</u> he/she
3. <u>Their</u> His/Her
4. <u>yourself</u> myself
5. <u>it</u> they

VI. 1. ours
2. Whose
3. your
4. theirs
5. its

VII. Answers will vary.

VIII. 1. matches
2. tests
3. knives
4. silver
5. bosses

IX. 1. C
2. himself
3. I
4. C
5. ourselves

Editing Practice:
Change you don't to he doesn't, you are to he is, you have to he has, and you to they

Chapter 2

Exercise 1A Answers will vary.

Exercise 1B
1. stops, stopped 2. hurries, hurried 3. trips, tripped 4. glare, glared
5. watches, watched

Exercise 1C Answers will vary.

Exercise 1D
1. plans 2. works 3. saves 4. opens 5. increases 6. waits
7. listens 8. changes 9. snows 10. anticipates

Exercise 2A
1. drive 2. see 3. comes 4. take 5. holds 6. throws
7. bends 8. hangs 9. brings 10. catch

Exercise 2B
1. met 2. came 3. gave 4. made 5. threw 6. rode
7. ate 8. had 9. held 10. kept

Group Activity
lived, enjoyed, watched, cleaned, toured, came, amused, saw, traveled,
asked, saw, shrugged, remarked, posed, looked, thought, understood,
disappointed, planned, tried

Exercise 2C
1. lays 2. sets 3. lies 4. sits 5. lay 6. sat 7. lying 8. lain 9. sat
10. sitting

Exercise 3A
1. stops, stopped, stopped, stopping 2. carries, carried, carried,
carrying 3. watches, watched, watched, watching 4. tries, tried, tried,
trying 5. hopes, hoped, hoped, hoping

Spelling Practice
1. letting 2. jumping 3. hitting 4. returning 5. sleeping
6. arriving 7. living 8. managing 9. blaming 10. competing

Exercise 3B
1. is, was/were, been, being 2. drives, drove, driven, driving 3. runs,
ran, run, running 4. chooses, chose, chosen, choosing 5. does, did,
done, doing

Exercise 4A
1. Can shop 2. might have received 3. would find 4. could send
5. can order 6. should appeal 7. may be surprised 8. must be filled out
9. will arrive 10. ought to shop

Exercise 4B Answers will vary.

Exercise 4C
1. have been helped 2. can see 3. can examine 4. may be done 5. must
cut 6. can be 7. are using 8. do think 9. are playing 10. Does seem

Exercise 4D Answers will vary.

Exercise 4E
1. run 2. become 3. thought 4. begun 5. taken 6. heard 7. found
8. made 9. seen 10. eaten

Exercise 4F
has (just) ended; have voted; have selected; had been complaining; said;
had (not) returned; had damaged; had been; returned; did (n't) want; did
(not) have; could do; are discussing

Exercise 4G
have built; must (often) share; are (now) surveying; are snatching; are accepting; have (also) appeared; had (even) found; was taking; would(n't) enjoy; was (finally) summoned; was(n't); was relocated; must (not) have seemed

Exercise 4H
1. are or were
2. have or had
3. have or had
4. have or had
5. will have

Exercise 5A
1. will begin 2. will set 3. will take 4. will be 5. will earn

Exercise 5B
1. will 2. would 3. will 4. would 5. will 6. would

Exercise 5C
1. will come 2. will need 3. would fill 4. will supply 5. would raise

Exercise 6A
1. has taught 2. has specialized 3. have enjoyed 4. has been 5. has done

Exercise 6B
1. had, read 2. had, promised 3. had had 4. had, enjoyed 5. had chosen

Exercise 6C
1. will have bought 2. will have read 3. will have made 4. will have started 5. will have returned

Exercise 6D
1. have spent 2. had spent 3. have bought 4. had purchased 5. will have saved 6. have found

Group Activity
(Answers, of course, may vary.) 1. He had asked Brian to stay late.
2. Brian knew that the manager had been watching him work.
3. Brian had never learned how to pack soft fruit.
4. Brian predicted that he would soon lose his job.

Lesson 7 Editing Practice
A. In 1975, Nga moved from a fishing village in Vietnam to a large city in southern Louisiana. She found the climate there similar to that of her native country. She and her husband settled in a suburb of New Orleans along with many other Vietnamese families. He worked as a fisherman, and she raised vegetables in a small garden plot. She faced difficulties adjusting to life in a strange land, but before long she

felt comfortable in her new home. In 1995, she and her husband proudly attended the college graduation ceremony of their daughter. Today that daughter works as a pharmacist in Atlanta, Georgia.
B. When my neighbor bought a used car, he received a lesson in odometer tampering. He thought he had bought a reliable, low-mileage car, but after he began driving it, problems developed. His mechanic told him that the car needed a new transmission although the odometer showed only 30,000 miles. The mechanic became suspicious. Worn brake and gas pedals suggested that the car had probably been driven over 75,000 miles. Scratches on the odometer further convinced the mechanic that the mileage had been changed.

Lesson 8 Suggested Sentences
A. Two hikers with heavy backpacks climbed the steep, rocky trail to Frog Lake. B. Another strip mall will eliminate our neighborhood park and increase traffic on our already crowded, narrow streets. C. During high school, Wynton Marsalis played first trumpet in the New Orleans Civic Orchestra. D. Delores has heard rock music and voices from the neighboring apartment all night long. E. A reporter interviewed a candidate for mayor in the coming election on a television news program last Friday.

Chapter Summary
1. third 2. -d, -ed 3. forms 4. will 5. have, past 6. be, do 7. adverbs
8. never, always, not

Practice Test
I.1. planned
2. spun
3. was
4. threw
5. offered

II.1. has completed
2. is campaigning
3. had
4. were shooting
5. do marry
6. have heard
7. Did complete
8. is
9. may need
10. had met

III. Sentences will vary.

IV. 1. will hold
2. will serve
3. will honor
4. would retire
5. would receive

V.1. had seen
2. has verified
3. has or had refused
4. had made
5. have convinced

VI.1. cries   cried cried crying
2. breaks broke broken breaking
3. is   was, were been being
4. tapes   taped taped taping
5. plans   planned planned planning

VII.1. has (always) been
2. Have (n't) (ever) gone
3. can (certainly) understand
4. has (recently) won
5. will (seldom) watch

Editing Practice:
Working in a legal office is a very demanding job. My job as a legal assistant consists of processing many felony complaints and other legal documents. These complaints must be filed in court; therefore, they have to be accurate and completed on time. I am working under pressure all the time. I have to be dependable and courteous. Even when I am tired and depressed, I still have to be helpful and polite.

Chapter 3

Exercise 1A
1. she 2. it 3. he 4. they 5. we

Exercise 1B

Subject	Auxiliary Verb	Main Verb
1. Americans	can	experience
2. festivals	are	held
3. We	have	attended
4. events	____	include
5. contestants	are	throwing
6. trials	____	show
7. collie	____	drives
8. Bagpipers	____	offer
9. They	have	led
10. you	may	think
you	____	are

Exercises 1C and 1D Answers will vary.

Exercise 2A

1. us 2. it 3. them 4. me 5. her

Exercise 2B

Subject	Verb	Object of Verb
1. scientists	created	transistor
2. transistor	did receive	attention
3. it	replaced	tubes
4. transistors	power	everything
5. Manufacturers	can place	millions

Exercise 2C Answers will vary.

Exercise 2D

1. read instructions
2. have been coming (no object)
3. is writing (no object)
4. did pass test
5. will (not) know results
6. Did(n't) post grades
7. Open door
8. has (not) completed assignment
9. is going (no object)
10. are driving (no object)

Exercise 3A

1. [to the Midwest] [in the United States] 2. [in the wilderness] [with no roads] 3. [by the time] [of the canal's opening] [of New York City] [of the state] 4. [between Albany and Buffalo] [to six days] [from two weeks] [by wagon] 5. [in 1825] [with the booming] [of a line] [of cannons] [along the way] [down the Hudson]

Exercise 3B

1. [to a baseball game] [along with two friends]
2. [contrary to the weather forecast]
3. [on account of the large crowd][at the box office]
4. [in front of us] [about the long wait][in line]
5. [After six innings] [because of rain]

Exercise 3C

1. The rangers [in Glacier National Park] must inform campers [about cow parsnip].
2. The cow parsnip, a member [of the parsley family,] is the favorite food [of the grizzly bears].
3. Grizzlies graze [like cattle] [on moist slopes] [of cow parsnips].
4. [At the time] [of year] when backpackers are entering the park [in large numbers,] the grizzlies are looking [for cow parsnips].
5. [According to the park rangers], the grizzly bears are never far [from the campers].
Subjects: 1. rangers 2. parsnip 3. Grizzlies 4. backpackers grizzlies
5. bears

9

Exercise 3D

Central Guitar <u>is</u> <u>located</u> [along with a number][of other guitar stores and studios][on one long block][in the middle of a large city]. Last month Jerry Montgomery, a college sophomore, <u>started</u> a part-time job [at Central]. Rock'n'roll music <u>has</u> always <u>been</u> one [of Jerry's enthusiasms], and his record collection <u>includes</u> artists [from Les Paul and Roy Orbison] [to Eddie Van Halen and The Wallflowers]. The store's customers <u>vary</u> widely. A beginning player [with only six weeks][of instruction] <u>may be</u> <u>standing</u> [in front of the counter][beside a star performer]. One <u>is</u> <u>shopping</u> [for a $95 guitar], and the other <u>admires</u> the finish [on a $20,000 instrument]. Autographed pictures [of the top rock stars] <u>decorate</u> the walls while the sound [of guitar music] <u>surges</u> [into the shop] [from the studios] [down the street]. Jerry <u>posts</u> a notice [of a rock concert][above a rack][of music] and <u>turns</u> [towards his next customer]. Jerry, [at this particular time], <u>has found</u> the perfect job.

Subjects: Central Guitar Jerry Montgomery music collection customers player One other pictures sound Jerry Jerry

Exercise 4A

1. Ballard earned 2. Davis founded 3. Davis commanded 4. airmen flew 5. flyers escorted 6. escorts lost (not one…) or escorts did not lose 7. Hall shot down 8. group bombed 9. performance strengthened 10. Tuskegee Airmen, Inc. assist

Lesson 4 Group Activity

A. 1. passive (was identified, was discovered) 2. active (whacked, knocked)
3. active (defied) and passive (was taken) 4. passive (was made) 5. passive
(was scattered) 6. passive (was honored) and active (won) 7. passive (is rumored, is being investigated) 8. passive(were uprooted)

Exercise 5A

	S	LV	C
1.	daughter	<u>is</u>	freshman
2.	She	<u>is</u>	physical education major
3.	light	<u>is</u> <u>turning</u>	green
4.	pedestrians	<u>seemed</u>	impatient
5.	you	<u>can</u> <u>be</u>	moderator
6.	discussion	<u>should</u> <u>be</u>	interesting
7.	Mrs. Chavez	<u>is</u>	friend
8.	Mrs. Chavez	<u>was</u>	friend and adviser

Exercises 5B Answers will vary.

Exercise 5C

Subject	Verb	Object/Completer
1. Marla	<u>has</u> <u>arrived</u>	no object
2. appointment	<u>was</u>	late
3. Jack	<u>has been</u> <u>waiting</u>	no object
4. They	<u>feel</u>	tired and hungry
5. refrigerator	<u>looks</u>	empty
6. Marla	<u>finds</u>	chicken
7. Jack	<u>makes</u> and <u>slices</u>	salad and bread

10

8. bread	<u>tastes</u>	stale
9. Marla	<u>prepares</u>	fruit
10. Jack	<u>does seem</u>	enthusiastic
11. Marla	<u>comes</u>	no object
12. She	<u>discovers</u>	pint

Group Activity

Although the achievements [of W.E.B. Du Bois] <u>were</u> many, his life <u>ended</u> sadly. Du Bois <u>was born</u> [in Massachusetts] [in 1868]. [Before the turn] [of the century], he <u>received</u> a doctorate [from Harvard University]. He <u>pioneered</u> experimental sociology [with *The Philadelphia Negro*], a book [about his interviews] [with thousands] [of Philadelphia natives]. [With that book], he <u>may have started</u> American sociology. Later, he <u>became</u> the editor [of *The Crisis*], the NAACP magazine. [Along the way], he <u>wrote</u> *The Souls* [*of the Black Folk*] and *Black Reconstruction* [*In America*]. He <u>clashed</u> [with Booker T. Washington], champion [of manual training] [for black youths]; [with Marcus Garvey], the black nationalist; and [with the National Association] [for the Advancement] [of Colored People]. [In the last years] [of his life], Du Bois <u>applied</u> [for membership] [in the Communist Party] and then <u>fled</u> [from America]. He <u>died</u> [in Ghana] [in 1963], a day [before the Rev. Martin Luther King's March] [on Washington]. [In the past,] W.E.B. Du Bois was <u>admired</u> [as teacher, model, and inspiration] [by many black scholars]. However, some scholars do not <u>admire</u> him today.

Subjects: achievements life Du Bois he He he he he He Du Bois He Du Bois scholars

Exercise 6A Answers will vary.

Exercise 6B
1. brother and I 2. <u>resented</u> and <u>complained</u> 3. language and customs
4. <u>wanted</u> and <u>envied</u> 5. Mother and Dad 6. interest and enjoyment
7. knowing and communicating 8. <u>attending</u> and <u>preparing</u> 9. Mother and Dad 10. <u>recall</u> and <u>smile</u>

Exercise 6C
1. her 2. me 3. her 4. him 5. We 6. her 7. he 8. him 9. I 10. me

Exercise 7A
1. she'll 2. they've 3. he'd 4. he's 5. I'll 6. I'm 7. we've 8. here's
9. it's 10. we're

Exercise 7B
A. 1. He'll 2. We'll 3. Here's 4. they're 5. There's 6. She'll 7. They'll
8. You're 9. Who's 10. We're
B.

Subject	Auxiliary Verb	Main Verb
2. We	will	shoot
3. basketball	____	is
4. they	are	going
5. entrance	____	is
6. She	will	be
7. They	will	have
8. You	are	wanted

11

| 9. Who | is | calling |
| 10. We | are | interested |

Lesson 8 Suggested Sentences
A. The members of the cast and the orchestra took their bows to the applause of the audience at the final performance of the play. B. The gardener finished his work, loaded his tools quickly on his truck, and drove off to his next job. C. In November my friend and I are going on a barge through the French countryside. D. The sports car skidded on the icy mountain road, spun around, and nearly rear-ended a huge truck. E. The frightened driver of the sports car turned the wheel sharply and brought the car to a skidding stop just in time.

Chapter Summary
1. verb, subject 2. prepositional 3. object 4. links 5. compound 6. "You"

Practice Test

Subject	Aux. Verb	Main Verb
I. 1. plates	have	expired
2. he	did	renew
3. (You)		pull
4. officer		listens
5. He	is	smiling and writing
6. Nola	has	been
7. She	had been	driving
8. library		is
9. school	is	held
10. class		met

II.1. <u>May</u> I <u>ride</u>[with you] [to school][on Wednesday]?   no object
2. <u>Write</u> the verbs[on the lines][at the right].   verbs
3. Eddie <u>will be</u> <u>working</u> [for a tax consultant][during March].   no object
4. The students[in the political science class]recently <u>heard</u> some startling facts.   facts
5. Tina <u>studies</u> French daily[from 10 A.M.][until noon].   French

III. Answers will vary.

IV. Answers will vary.

V. 1. I
2. She
3. me
4. him
5. He

VI. 1. with her coach	for many months	
2. Despite the pain	in her arm	to the court
3. After a half hour	on her shoulder	
4. together with her coach	around the track	in the afternoon
5. in the tournament	because of the injured shoulder	

VII. a. 1. We'll
2. They're
3. You're
4. I've
5. You'll

Subject	Aux. Verb	Main Verb
VII. b. 1.We	will	help
2. They		are
3. You	are	going
4. I	have been	looking
5. You	will	get

Editing Practice
1. He and I 2. him and me 3. he and I 4. you and me 5. she and her partner 6. my brother and I
7. my brother and I

Chapter 4

Exercise 1A
1. reserved, fought 2. paper 3. home, closing, 4. rookie, scoring 5. sports, winning 6. nylon, leather, wool 7. Alex's, crowded, 8. stadium, Alex's, no-parking

Exercise 1B Answers will vary.

Exercise 1C
1. scenic, rugged 2. purple, red, and blue-gray 3. Steep red...clear, intense 4. mineralized, rainbow-colored 5. remarkable, breathtaking, and memorable

Group Activity
Part A
It is [a] [beautiful], [sunny] day in [a] [popular] [theme] park in [the] United States. Mr. and Mrs. Tomita, on [their] [first] trip to [this] country, listen attentively to [a] [tour guide's] claim that [thirty-five thousand] adults and children visit [the] park [every] day. [Most] visitors to [this] [magical] place are attracted by [an] [amazing] variety of shows, rides, exhibits, and restaurants. [Both] Mr. and Mrs. Tomita, however, are impressed by [the] [clean] surroundings. They are staying at [the] [vacationland's] hotel where [the] rooms have immaculately [clean], [blue] [plastic] furniture, [green] and [beige] walls, and beds [covered] with [purple-green] spreads. [The] [hotel's] [parking] lot, with [its] carefully [planted] vegetation, is also [sparkling] and [clean]. [The] [smallest] scrap of litter is sucked underground and rushed via pipes to [an] [efficient] [trash] compactor. Even [the] [friendly] birds do [their] part by picking [some] [bread] crumbs off [the] [restaurant's] patio at [the] hotel. Mr. and Mrs. Tomita know that they will enjoy themselves in [this] [spotless] [American] [tourist] attraction.

Part B Sentences will vary.

Exercise 2A Answers will vary.

Exercise 2B
1. perfectly 2. well 3. easily 4. good 5. smoothly 6. really 7. well 8. bad 9. quickly 10. seriously

Exercise 2C
A. The bookstore was having a sale of slightly soiled, reduced books, but the delighted customers didn't mind the smudge marks.
B. Books and magazines filled the salesman's large, brown leather briefcase.
C. Ervin's bicycle is lightweight, but it is strong enough to ride on paved city streets and unpaved country roads.
D. On Monday the new foreign minister arrived early in the morning in Helsinki.
E. On Sunday afternoons, Mrs. Konitz usually joined her friends on the same bench just inside the gate at the south end of the park.

Exercise 3A 2. easier 3. better 4. bigger, more powerful 5. most recent 6. greater 7. more efficient 8. simpler *or* more simple 9. largest 10. best, lowest

Exercise 3B
2. more efficiently 3. more systematically 4. more easily 5. better 6. most often 7. most significantly

Exercise 3C 1. less 2. least 3. less 4. least 5. less.

Exercise 3D Answers will vary.

Exercise 3E
1. most enthusiastic 2. more active 3. youngest 4. highest 5. more unusual 6. most important

Group Activity Part A.
A baseball can carry [farther] in some stadiums than in others. Most hitters [already] know that fact. There is [also] evidence that, on some days and in some stadiums, a ball will go [even] [farther]. The ideal day would be [very] hot and [very] humid. The stadium in Denver, located at an altitude of 5280 feet, is the ideal place. Many players hit [best] of all in Denver's stadium, and they hit [worst] of all in the stadium in San Diego. The stadium in that city is at sea level, and there is [almost] no humidity. A baseball travels [fastest] and [farthest] on hot, humid days and at high altitudes. So if you are [seriously] interested in becoming a "home-run king," you should travel to Denver on an [exceptionally] hot day in August, and you should be able to hit the ball [harder] and [faster].

Group Activity Part B. Sentences will vary.

Exercise 4A Answers will vary.

Exercise 4B
The water [in the Amazon] is muddy. It is hard [to see just a few feet down], and twenty feet down, it is impossible [to see anything]. But electric fish are able [to navigate] [at that depth] [without vision]. They use electric organs [to generate electric fields] [around their bodies] [to sense other living things]. Catfish, [using feelers], probe the muddy waters. They also have taste buds all [over their bodies], [allowing other senses] [to dominate] [over sight]. Researchers have found many

14

eyeless fish [swimming at the bottom] [of the Amazon]. They survive [by eating the tails] [of other fish]. The fish can then grow new tails.

Another unusual group [of fish] [found in the Amazon] survive [by eating dead wood] [found along the banks] [of the river]. [Hoping to discover] more rare species, researchers are dragging nets [along the bottom] [of the muddy river] [to bring them] [to the surface] [for study]. The nets have brought in a tiny transparent catfish that is only one-third [of an inch] long. It is also blind, but it has thickened bones and armored plates [on its side] [to protect it] [from larger fish]. So far, the waters [of the Amazon] are estimated [to harbor] at least 200 million fish species. That number is nearly twice the number [of fish species] [in all] [of North America].

Answers to questions will vary.

Exercise 4C
1. Hoping to make a profit, Carolyn…
2. Trying to get to the airport on time, Josephine…
3. Snowed in for a week in the mountains, we…
4. Having spent the day shopping unsuccessfully for shoes, Tina…
5. Finding a wallet on his way to school, Jerry…

Exercise 5A
1. Nick saved almost $100 by making his own repairs on his car.
2. The candidate promised at the political rally that he would reduce unemployment.
3. Alfredo ordered a pizza with mushrooms and pepperoni to go.
4. The painters told us on Wednesday that they would begin painting the house.
or The painters told us that they would begin painting the house on Wednesday.
5. Rex suddenly saw a woman in the front row jump up and run out ... exit.
or Rex ... jump up suddenly ... exit.

Exercise 5B
1. Everyone noticed the new police unit in town, Barney and Fred, riding around in a black and white patrol car marked K-9 Patrol.
2. Barney drove the car, and Fred, sitting in the back seat, was, unfortunately, a bit too eager for action.
3. Stopping the car at a traffic light or an intersection, Barney would hear Fred's growls.
4. Putting his head out of the window, Fred frequently snarled and barked at pedestrians who passed close to the car.
5. In their complaints to the police department, disgruntled citizens said that Fred was supposed to protect them, not attack them.
6. The police chief, hoping to restore peace and order, sent Barney and Fred back to training classes.
7. Trained to control his enthusiasm, Fred was no longer an embarrassment to Barney.
8. Now when Barney stops the patrol car, Fred sits calmly in the back seat, facing the front of the car.
9. Only his eyes move--from left to right and from right to left.
10. He doesn't even bark at the cats that he sees on the prowl.

Exercise 5C Answers will vary.

Editing Practice Answers will vary.

Lesson 6 Suggested Sentences

A. Late summer thunderstorms flooded the region with more than seventeen inches of rain in places, sending hundreds of people to higher ground.

B. The determined opponents, writing over 500 letters and circulating a petition, stirred up public opinion against the location of the chemical plant.

C. Julia told us about her recent trip to China, especially emphasizing the part about the exciting boat ride up the Yangtze River.

D. Sage Ranch was a popular movie location with its big red boulders that served two purposes by sheltering the good guys camping out and concealing the bad guys hiding out.

E. Located on the Bay of Naples, the ancient city of Pompeii was destroyed by an earthquake in AD 79.

Chapter Summary

1. what kind, how many, which one 2. comparative, superlative 3. verbs, adjectives, adverbs
4. how, when, where, why 5. misplaced modifiers

Practice Test

I.			
1. The	three	gold
2. Scrambled	that	Teflon
3. her	ex-husband's	good
4. The	any	damaged
5. His	smudged	illegible

II. 1. suddenly
2. frequently
3. n't
4. politely
5. just

III. 1. most energetic
2. better
3. worst
4. most competitive
5. more expert

IV. 1. most intelligently
2. hardest
3. better
4. more prudently
5. worse

V. 1. Some of the parents, angered by the new busing plan, shouted at the members of the school board.
2. I knew that the bicycle tire, leaking air slowly, would soon be flat.
3. Without much hope, the defendant watched the jury return with its verdict.

VI. 1. As I was looking at the opposite shore, the telescope brought the waterfront buildings into focus.
2. When I was only two years old, my uncle took me to see my first major-league baseball game.

3. While Tricia was eating lunch, the orange squirted juice all over her new silk blouse.

Editing Practice

Errors	Corrections
real	really
powerfulest	most powerful
more impressed	most impressed
most grandest	grandest
more better	better
badly	bad
spectacularest	most spectacular

Chapter 5

Exercise 1A
1. phrase 2. main clause 3. phrase 4. main clause 5. phrase

Exercise 1B Answers will vary.

Exercise 2A

Subject	Auxiliary Verb	Verb	Type of Sentence
1. people	_____	think	
bicyclists	_____	know	compound
2. bicyclists	_____	ride	simple
3. ride	_____	begins	
it	_____	ends	compound
4. riders	_____	complain	simple
5. bicyclists	are	surprised	
land	had	looked	compound

Exercise 2B
1. year, yet of these,… 2. spawn, so they… 3. path, but others… 4. lore, and thus, he… 5. water, for these Seminoles…

Exercise 2C
1. Compound: streets; instead,… 2. Simple 3. Compound: New York; she is… 4. Compound: metropolis; no other… 5. Simple

Exercise 2D Answers will vary.

Exercise 2E
1. twelve; consequently, this 2. pilot; then, he 3. miner; instead, he
4. gentleman; in addition, he 5. behind; in fact, Hannibal

Exercise 2F
1. A dictionary, indeed, 2. Besides that, a 3. dictionary, in addition, shows 4. you, furthermore, the
5. dictionary, in fact, is 6. Moreover, if you 7. You should, in fact, keep 8. Thus, you will have 9. You must, however, develop

Exercise 2G

1. Alan always wanted to play in the Rose Bowl, but his team's...
2. Alan's team will try harder next year, so perhaps ...
3. Playing in the Rose Bowl is every football player's dream; however, few...
4. On New Year's Day Alan will watch the game on TV; his teammates will be there too.

Group Activity

Paragraph on the European satellite

1. Simple Sentences: 1, 4, 5
2. Compound Sentences: 2, 3
3. Coordinating Connectives are in sentences 2 and 3: but, and
4. Prepositional and Verbal Phrases: 12 as follows:

   In 1989   to measure the position   of 120,000 stars   to reach its correct orbit   after its launching   from the ground   since 1993   by its findings   to change their thinking   about the size   of the universe   than the previous estimates

Answers to questions 5 through 8 will vary.

Editing Practice

1. <u>to drive too fast</u> 2. <u>that I should go on a diet</u> 3. <u>the worry about finances</u> 4. <u>to learn how to play tennis</u> 5. <u>was parking her car in the parking lot.</u>

1. driving too fast 2. to go on a diet 3. worrying about finances 4. to take tennis lessons 5. parked her car

Exercise 3A Sentences will vary.

Exercise 3B

1. subjects: the sea, the woods, and the mountains. 2. life: young couples at a picnic, an ice skating party on a pond, and a berry-picking expedition in the woods. 3. They sit on rail fences, share watermelons, raid sand-swallow nests, and build a fire for a clambake on the beach. 4. their parents unload boats, mend gear, and haul in nets of fish. 5. the power, the danger, the violence, and the beauty of the spectacle.

Exercise 4A

Some suggestions for corrections:

1. The long line of weather watchers, turning for assistance from birds, <u>may have</u> <u>begun</u> with Noa**h, for** he <u>sent</u> out a raven and a dove from the ark, hoping for an end to the long rain.   CS
2. According to some, the distinctive calls of woodpeckers and robins <u>signal</u> rai**n; however**, the unusual silence of other birds supposedly <u>makes</u> the same prediction.   RO
3. Hawks, perched high on power poles, <u>are</u> another indicator of coming rai**n;** they <u>wait</u> to catch small creatures heading from low creek beds to the safety of higher ground.   RO
4. On some days, seagulls <u>remain</u> on the shore, seeming to avoid the ocea**n; in fact,** fishermen once <u>took</u> the gulls' behavior as a sign of a coming storm and also <u>stayed</u> in port.   CS
5. Birds themselves <u>are</u> weather watchers during the time for migratio**n;** needing good weather to navigate, they <u>postpone</u> their departure during uncertain weather conditions.   RO

Subjects: 1. line he 2. calls silence 3. Hawks they 4. seagulls fishermen 5. Birds they

Exercise 4B

Some suggestions for corrections:

1. More corporations are beginning to open day-care centers for their employees' children**, and** the centers are open from nine to five.

2. With their children in these centers, working parents worry less about the**m; therefore,** these parents take fewer days off.

3. Two-paycheck families appreciate the cost benefits**; in fact,** the price of a full-time baby-sitter would use up an entire salary.

4. Single-parent families especially appreciate the convenience of quality child-care programs**, for** child-care programs help to recruit high-quality employees.

5. Government support helps the corporations build special facilitie**s; p**reschool playgrounds and indoor classrooms are often too expensive for smaller corporations to construct.

Editing Practice

Some suggestions for corrections:

1. addicts; each year
2. world; however,
3. publication, and it
4. thriving; in fact,
5. friend, for

Lesson 5 Suggested Sentences

A. Looking for a job in the rapidly growing computer field, Shana sent her résumé to software developers, manufacturing companies, and health maintenance organizations.

B. Astronomers have known about five planets in our solar system for centuries, but an astronomer at Lowell Observatory in Arizona did not discover Pluto until 1930.

C. Walking onto one of Tokyo's new commuter trains, Keiko notices a television screen above the door; the screen shows, in English as well as Japanese, the current stop, the next stop, and also gives some news and commercials.

D. Calling a press conference on Friday, the governor announced his education plan to provide more computers for schools, to reduce class size, and to expand the intern program for teachers.

Chapter Summary

1. subject 2. main 3. compound 4. semicolon 5. parallel

Practice Test

I. 1. MC
2. P
3. P
4. MC
5. MC

II. 1. compound
2. simple
3. simple
4. simple
5. compound

III. 1. compound ; however,
2. simple ,meanwhile,
3. compound ;in addition,
4. compound ;consequently,
5. simple ,therefore,

IV. 1. <u>lamps made of brass</u> brass lamps 2. <u>an atmosphere that is pleasant</u> a pleasant atmosphere
3. <u>To know the techniques of marketing</u> knowing the techniques of marketing 4. <u>coaches her daughter's soccer team</u> but also is her daughter's soccer team coach 5. <u>opening new company offices there</u> to open new company offices there.

V. Suggested answers:
1. tonight, or we (CS)
2. music; Howard (RO)
3. CDs; however, (CS)
4. weeks, but (RO)
5. high; therefore, (CS)

Editing Practice
Examples of parallel structure are as follows:
1. You have studied the store's advertisements, and you have decided exactly what color and size you need.
2. Finally, disappointed, you give up, return your credit card to your wallet, and head for the exit.
3. Or else,…what item you want to buy nor where to find it in the store.
4. Retailers deny that they have reduced their sales staff, but they do admit that they have reduced their sales costs.
5. That translates to fewer salespeople on the floor and fewer well-trained people to serve you.
6. Of course,…cannot count on careful attention in the lingerie department, knowledgeable service in the fine china department, or cheerful service at the lunch counter.

Chapter 6

Exercise 1A
1. _____
2. x
3. x
4. _____

Exercise 1B
1. after
2. when
3. although
4. because
5. before
Sentences will vary.

Exercises 1C and 1D Answers will vary.

Exercise 1E

Japanese women <u>who</u> were enthusiastic buyers of expensive imported goods <u>when</u> times were good, have turned to "recycle shops," <u>which</u> offer used luxury items at reduced prices. <u>Although</u> a young Japanese woman may have less money to spend during these years of recession, she hasn't lost her desire for a Gucci handbag <u>whose</u> original price may have been $800. Their grandmothers, concerned with cleanliness and the possibility <u>that</u> the spirit of the former owners remained with their possessions, avoided secondhand objects, but these young women seem undisturbed by such concerns. The stores <u>where</u> they shop formerly were pawn shops <u>that</u> were located in back alleys. <u>Because</u> they hope to attract an entirely different clientele, owners of these stores have redecorated them and restocked them with used luxury brand names. <u>Since</u> many young Japanese women live at home, they can spend up to 90% of their income on luxuries. Consequently, they shop <u>wherever</u> they can find a $200 dress or accessory at the discount price of $30.

Exercise 1F

1. <u>(When) the Aztecs arrived in the Valley of Mexico in 1325</u>, they <u>became</u> farmers <u>(who) were forced to create their farmland artificially</u>.
2. They <u>settled</u> on an island <u>(that) was in the middle of Lake Texcoco</u>, and <u>(after) they dredged mud from the bottom of the lake</u>, they <u>piled</u> it along the shores to create "floating" gardens.
3. <u>(Since) water continuously seeped up through the mud</u>, the soil <u>was kept</u> moist, allowing plants to grow and protecting the crops from drought <u>(before) the rainy season began.</u>
4. <u>(As) the Aztec population expanded</u>, the "floating" gardens <u>were used</u> for urban development, <u>(while) food production was moved to the southern end of the valley</u>.
5.   The Aztecs' settlement <u>developed</u> into a city of thousands of small islands <u>(which) were divided by canals (that) formed the basis of their transportation system.</u>
Subjects: 1. Aztecs they who 2. They that they they 3. water soil season 4. population gardens production 5. settlement which that

Group Activity

Do you know <u>(what) a kiwi is</u>? It is a plum-sized fruit <u>(that) has become popular all over America.</u> <u>(When) you look at the outside</u>, you see a dull brown, fuzzy exterior. <u>(When) you cut it open</u>, the fruit is bright green and fragrant. <u>(While) some people (who) have tasted it think (that) it tastes like a banana</u>, others find the flavor hard to describe. It is considered nutritious <u>(because) it contains more vitamin C (than) an orange does</u>. Kiwi growers also say <u>(that) the juice can be sprinkled on tough meat as a tenderizer</u>. <u>(Although) it was first cultivated in China about 300 years ago</u>, it was not known in the western hemisphere until the twentieth century. Now, most kiwis come from New Zealand <u>(where) they grow all year round</u>. <u>(If) you have not tasted a kiwi yet</u>, you may be in for a surprise. They are, however, quite expensive, so they may strain your budget <u>(while) they tingle your tastebuds.</u>

Exercise 2A

1. (When) Blanche attended a lab technician's convention in Vancouver, British Columbia
2. (Because) she came from a small town in Missouri
3. (which) caused the sunlight to sparkle
4. (when) they reflected the dazzling sunlight
5. (where) enormous totem poles overwhelmed the large ...
6. (who) had carved them
7. (who) enjoyed the view of Vancouver framed by the mountains
8. (After) she drove to Queen Elizabeth Park
9. (because) she wanted to eat at the Teahouse Restaurant

10. (where) she sat outdoors ...
11. (so that) she could look back at the city's skyline ...
12. (Before) she left Vancouver
13. (which) she brought back to her family in Missouri.
Sentences will vary.

Exercise 2B
1. Although spiders are of great benefit to our environment, many people, unfortunately, dislike and
fear them.   RO
2. While several species are quite poisonous, these represent...   RO
3. Spiders are invaluable to us since they devour...   CS
4. According to many scientists, spiders keep the balance of nature because,
without spiders, these...   CS
5. Spiders, in general, appear in a favorable light when they appear...   RO
Other sentences may also be correct.

Exercise 2C
1. Although many people might laugh at the idea of computers belonging in every classroom,
others will accept the reality.
2. While some critics prefer an excellent teacher, many would vote for an excellent multimedia
computer system.
3. Generations of pupils who have learned from textbooks are protesting against the expense of
electronic installations. (no comma needed)
4. If you wanted to improve the quality of education in America, you would keep computers out of
the classroom.
5. That slogan has been adopted by those parents whose children need more textbooks, teachers,
and traditional values. (no comma needed)

Exercise 2D
1. The sled dog race that is run between Whitehorse and Fairbanks should not be confused with the
more widely publicized Iditarod. (no comma needed)
2. The Iditarod Trail Sled Dog Race, which is a 1,150-mile race in Alaska from Anchorage to Nome,
began in 1973.
3. The race that is known as the Yukon Quest International Sled Dog Race made its first appearance
in 1983 and covers about 1,060 miles. (no comma needed)
4. The fifteen mushers who complete the race share a purse of $125,000. (no comma needed)
5. Promoters of the Yukon Quest, which shares many similarities with the Iditarod, maintain that
their race is more challenging and less commercial than its competitor.
6. Both races are endurance contests in the subarctic wilderness, which test both human and canine
ability to face the extreme hardships and isolation imposed by the courses.

Exercises 3A and 3B Sentences will vary.

Exercise 3C
1. S 2. F 3. S 4. F 5. F 6. F 7. S 8. F 9. F 10. F Sentences will vary.

Lesson 4 Suggested Sentences
A. I still remember the fear of looking down at the earth and leaping into space, and I remember
the joy of landing safely and seeing my buddies. B. As I float gently downward, I'm afraid that

22

I'll land in the river with eighty pounds of equipment on my back. C. When I fall to the ground on the river bank, I gather and bury my chute in the nearby jungle before I run to the waiting truck. D. We are alone now in enemy territory, with only our skills to keep us alive, although we have walkie-talkies to keep us in touch with our commanders.

Chapter Summary
1. sentence 2. complex 3. subordinate 4. subordinator 5. attach 6. subject 7. auxiliary

Practice Test
I. 1. [Although] <u>Mr. Barr tried to stop in time</u>
2. [who] <u>changed lanes abruptly</u>
3. [because] <u>he always remembered to "buckle up."</u>
4. [When] <u>he saw the damage to his car</u>
5. [who] <u>had only minor bruises</u>

II. A. and B. Answers will vary.

III. Answers will vary.

IV. 1. (RO) If Morgan's TV reception is poor, he may have to install a satellite TV antenna.
2. (CS) The Picasso painting that is valued at $10 million was bought by a Japanese investor.
3. (CS) Megan bought a new car so that she can have reliable transportation.
4. (RO) We may as well buy a new dishwasher as long as we are remodeling the kitchen.
5. (RO) Many listeners who enjoy listening to National Public Radio show their appreciation by giving financial support to their local stations.

V.A. 1. S
2. F
3. S
4. F
5. F
6. S
7. S
8. S
9. F
10. S
11. F
12. S

V. B. Answers will vary. Suggested sentences:
1. Muzak is difficult to escape unless city dwellers stay out of many public places, such as shopping malls, supermarkets, offices, restaurants, and elevators.
2. Even if they do, Muzak invades their homes via the telephone when they are put "on hold" while waiting for the completion of a call.
3. Although most people hear canned music almost daily, few of them actually listen to it.
4. The musical selections have always been carefully chosen to blend into the background of any activity by playing well-known tunes that would appeal to a mass audience.
5. This music is intended to make people feel good in the belief that they will then be productive workers and willing buyers.

Editing Practice Fragments are underlined as follows:

Pirates are often pictured as inhuman. <u>Quick to kill someone in pursuit of treasure</u>. In movies and novels, they often sank helpless ships. <u>Forcing prisoners to walk the plank</u>. But scholars in recent years have said that most of the mythology is wrong or misleading. They were less cruel and more democratic than previously thought. They carefully divided up the distribution among crew members. <u>Including rare jewelry from the African gold trade</u>. From recent finds on pirate ships located on the ocean bottom, scientists have learned that real pirates had no time for such ceremonies. <u>As sending victims walking down the plank</u>. They imprisoned some sailors and even treated them well. Also, pirates were not exclusively European. Perhaps as many as 30% of them were black slaves who had escaped from captivity. <u>Or been freed by pirate gangs to join in the attacks on organized trade</u>. These crews had established democratic principles aboard ship. Even the most feared captain, the famous Captain Blackbeard, shared equally with the members of the crew. <u>As he could not receive a larger portion of the booty</u>. Blackbeard's ship has now been located off the coast of Beaufort, N. C. <u>Where it had lain since 1718</u>. When the divers searched that ship, they hoped to find further proof of the lack of accuracy in the typical portrayal of pirates.

Suggested Corrections

Pirates are . . .inhuman, quick to kill someone in pursuit of treasure.

In movies. . .helpless ships, forcing prisoners to walk the plank.

They carefully. . .members, including rare jewelry from the African gold trade.

From recent. . .for such ceremonies as sending victims walking down the plank.

Perhaps as many. . .captivity or been freed by pirate gangs to join in the attacks on organized trade.

Even the most. . .crew as he could not receive a larger portion of the booty.

Blackbeard's ship. . .Beaufort, N.C., where it had lain since 1718.

Chapter 7

Exercise 1A and Exercise 1B Sentences will vary.

Exercise 2A

Subjects	Aux. Verbs and Main Verbs	Words Between Subject and Verb
2. Zookeeper	works	(whenever possible)
3. species	are bred	(such as the condor)
4. animals	seem	(released into their natural habitats)
5. zoo	plays	(in the country)
6. zoos	conduct	(that have the money, space, and time)

Exercise 2B

Subject	Verb
1. effects	linger
2. trees	have withered
3. flowers	are turning
4. farmers	are using
5. hope	is

Exercise 2C

Subject	Verb
1. disagreement	is
2. much	is
3. chances	are
4. clue	is
5. humidity	signals
6. devices	are
7. device	is
8. problem	is
9. way	is
10. appliances	are

Exercise 2D Sentences will vary.

Exercises 2E Sentences will vary.

Exercise 2F
1. have 2. have 3. have 4. have 5. has 6. has

Exercise 2G Sentences will vary.

Exercise 3A
Subjects: 1. No one 2. everyone 3. nobody 4. Neither 5. each 6. either
Verbs: 1. needs 2. works 3. takes 4. receives 5. depends 6. plans

Exercise 3B Sentences will vary.

Exercise 3C
1. is 2. was 3. has 4. was 5. includes

Exercise 3D Sentences will vary.

Exercise 3E

Antecedents	Verbs
1. Americans	seek
2. family	goes
3. DVDs	plug
4. video games	hook
5. television	has

Group Activity
A. The blossoming of the cherry [trees] (that) <u>surround</u> the Jefferson Memorial on the Tidal Basin is one of the loveliest signs of spring in the nation's capital. The 3,700 [trees] of several varieties, (which) <u>were</u> a gift of Japan in 1912, grow in two parks in Washington, D.C. Most of the [trees], (which) <u>are</u> the Yoshino variety, produce a white, cloud-like blossom, while the Akebonos, fewer in number, contribute a delicate pink to the sea of color, appearing briefly for two weeks each year. A weeklong [Cherry Blossom Festival], (which) <u>opens</u> with the lighting of a 300-year-old, 8-½-foot Japanese stone lantern, includes a parade and many other activities. The

blossoms, as might be expected, do not appear on schedule every year on a specific day; the time ranges somewhere between March 15, the earliest date, and April 18, the latest one recorded. The hundreds of thousands of [tourists], (who) <u>arrive</u> in expectation of the event, will be disappointed if the trees do not flower during their visit. Moreover, the festival [plans], (which) <u>await</u> completion, depend upon the estimated blossoming time.

The [question] (that) <u>arises</u> for most of us concerns how the date can be predicted with a high degree of accuracy. Fortunately, the National Parks Service [horticulturist], (who) <u>seems</u> to use a combination of art and science to make his prediction, is equal to the task. Beginning in late February, when the small red buds begin to appear, he makes daily visits to observe the trees, watching for the change in the buds from a tight red to a puffy white. He also considers two [factors,] daylight and temperature (which) <u>affect</u> the blooming time. In general, the length of daylight tells plants when to blossom, and there are some [biologists] (who) <u>feel</u> daylight is a more reliable factor than temperature. The horticulturist has learned, however, that local temperature plays a special role in regard to cherry trees. Warm days with no snow on the ground will bring an earlier bloom than the same temperature accompanied by snow on the ground. He suggests that the trees are, in effect, standing with their "feet" in ice water although the days are warm. In this way, he estimates the week of peak bloom quite accurately to the satisfaction of the festival personnel and a great many [people] (who<u>) arrive</u> from out of town.

B. and C. Answers will vary.

Exercise 4A

Pronouns	Antecedents
1. their	Matt and Richard
2. his	Jaime
3. her	Neither Jan nor Theresa
4. their	Mr. and Mrs. Asano
5. their	students

Exercise 4B
1. its 2. its 3. its 4. their 5. its

Exercise 4C

Pronoun	Antecedents	Possible Revisions
1. his or her	Someone	Someone left those books on the desk.
2. his or her	anyone	Has anyone brought a camera?
3. her	each	
4. his or her	Nobody	Nobody has received the final grades in the mail yet.
5. his or her	Everyone	All employees must show their badges to the guard at the gate.

Sentences will vary.

Exercise 4D
1. who 2. that 3. who 4. that 5. that

Exercise 4E
1. Jacquie said to Tess, "I have lost my pen."(Or) Jacquie mentioned that Tess had lost her pen.
2. There are so many automobile accidents because drivers are careless.

3. Charles Brocard is a marine archaeologist. Marine archaeology is a new and challenging profession.
4. Juan told Bob, "Your car needs repainting." (Or) According to Juan, Bob's car needs repainting.
5. In some parts of Canada the people speak French.

Lesson 5 Suggested Sentences
A. The Canadian geese population has increased so rapidly that the marshland where they normally find food has been destroyed by their digging through the soil surface to find food. B. As I was walking down an unpaved Alaskan road on a late summer afternoon, I whistled a cheerful tune to frighten away any hungry bears. C. The Lighthouse of Pharos, which is one of the Seven Wonders of the Ancient World, stands like a sentinel on the island of Pharos in the harbor of Alexandria, Egypt. D. Marian Anderson, who experienced racial prejudice during her early years, became the first African-American singer to join the Metropolitan Opera and to receive the Presidential Medal of Freedom.

Chapter Summary
1. subject 2. pronoun 3. follows 4. plural 5. singular 6. singular 7. singular 8. antecedents

Practice Test
I. 1. objects 2. were 3. have 4. have 5. seems

II. 1. is 2. was 3. learns 4. need 5. seems

III. 1. they 2. her 3. its 4. its 5. their

IV. 1. Marsha called her mother once a week when Marsha was out of town.
2. The doctor returned his patient's call before the doctor went to lunch.
3. The Parks Department should make pedestrians and roller skaters stay off the bike path.
4. Jared is studying marine biology. Marine biology is a rewarding profession.
5. When Daniel turned in a late research paper, his history instructor was annoyed.

V. Answers will vary.

VI. 1. Hal Prince. who won a Tony award last year. will direct the new musical.
2. The director, who was pleased with the actors' performances that day, called for one more rehearsal.
3. When the actors heard the announcement, they all cheered.
4. No commas
5. The new play, which was opening in New York, was sure to be a hit.

Editing Practice

Errors	Corrections
1. their harbor	its harbor
2. Here is the ruins	Here are the ruins
3. have exchanged	has exchanged
4. There was 3,500 dives	There were 3,500 dives
5. paid his respects	paid their respects
6. were destined to enjoy	was destined to enjoy
7. comes some major	come some major

8. <u>favors</u> leaving   <u>favor</u> leaving

9. <u>propose</u> making   <u>proposes</u> making

Sentences in answer to the questions will vary.

Chapter 8

Exercise 1A
1. food, but
2. pigments, and
3. compound, and
4. pigment, or
5. pink, but

Exercise 1B

The unnecessary commas have been removed in this paragraph.

The government has spent billions of dollars to protect our shorelines from the destruction of storms, but coastal geologists maintain that these efforts only accelerate the damage. Engineers build structures such as jetties or breakwaters, yet they fail to stop the erosion. Geologists say that this policy is based on a misunderstanding for all the engineers' good intentions. Beaches do not need these barriers and actually provide protection for the continent. Sand builds up in sand dunes when the ocean is calm, and waves move this sand out to the sea bottom during a storm. Beaches then become flatter, so waves break earlier and cause less erosion. Beaches that have neither seawalls nor bulkheads to interrupt the natural cycle rebuild their defenses as calmer waters carry the sand back to the shore. Miles of east-coast beaches have disappeared after 70 years of engineered beach construction, and the loss can only continue if the advice of geologists is ignored.

Exercise 2A Sentences will vary.

Exercise 2B

1. filmmaker, and composer 2. photographs, an art show 3. in excellent, inexpensive condition 4. Kansas, Minnesota 5. photojournalism, documentaries, and fashion photography 6. segregated, restrictive 7. poverty, prejudice, and injustices

Exercise 3A

The commas in sentences 2, 3, 4, and 7 are optional.

1. Among the staples of southwestern cooking, the chile is probably the most essential.
2. By the way, New Mexicans spell "chile" with a final "e" not an "i."
3. In addition, the chile is not actually a pepper as Columbus believed when he "discovered" it on one of his voyages.
4. In fact, the capsicum (chile) is a distant cousin of the tomato and is classified by botanists as a fruit.
5. Ranging from mild to incredibly hot, the chile's color depends on when it is harvested.
6. Produced by the same plant, green chilies are picked early and red chilies late in the season after they have matured.
7. Moreover, color is no guide to pungency; red or green sauce can be mild or hot depending on each specific batch.
8. While eating a food flavored with the chile, you may suddenly need to put out the fire, but eat something sweet or creamy instead of reaching for a glass of ice water.

Exercise 3B
1.Yes 2. No 3. comma optional 4. Yes 5. Yes 6. comma optional

Editing Practice
Although a comet looks very beautiful as it sails across the sky, it is not much more than a dirty snowball. A comet consists of chunks of rocky or metallic material, dust, and ice. While the ice is mainly frozen water, it also contains a mixture of methane, ammonia, and carbon dioxide molecules. When a comet passes close to the sun, it loses some of its matter. Some of its ice turns to a gas form as a comet nears the sun. The gases spread out around the nucleus, forming a large, thin atmosphere called a "coma," which glows in the sunlight. If the supply of gases from the nucleus changes, a comet can brighten and fade noticeably. As a comet approaches the sun, a solar wind sweeps a comet's gases away from the sun. So a second tail consisting of dust particles may also appear. Although this dust tail is shorter than the gas tail, it may also be visible from Earth. In fact, some comets have been observed to have as many as nine tails.

Exercise 4A
1. remove comma 2. Yes 3. Yes 4. insert comma after Asheville 5. Yes 6. Yes 7. insert comma after cities

Group Activity
Geothermal heat may be a new source of energy for **us,** but it is an ancient means of providing power by tapping a natural resource. Subsidized by federal grants and tax **advantages,** developers have tripled the use of geothermal power. In many western states **today,** communities are hoping to reduce their dependence on fossil fuels by utilizing this alternative energy source where it is available. Since geothermal heat is a fairly economical source of **power,** it has a growing number of supporters. Boise, Idaho, has become well known among proponents of this form of energy because this city has taken advantage of the hot wells underneath it. Boise has laid pipes beneath its streets to heat **restaurants, shops, business offices,** and the state office buildings. This old-new source of power can supply only a small part of the nation's energy **needs,** but it can provide a substantial savings to those regions possessing this natural advantage. Answers to the questions will vary.

Exercise 5A
1. In the early morning, the joggers run effortlessly along the deserted, shell-strewn beach.
2. Even on gray, foggy, chilly mornings, they wear only tank tops and brief running shorts.
3. Bicycle riders on the nearby, winding concrete bike path must be alert as jogging parents push their small children in vehicles especially constructed for this purpose.
4. Some cyclists are also accompanied by their youngsters riding in low, plastic-curtained trailers attached to the back of the bikes.
5. When the morning overcast begins to burn off, the second shift appears: volleyball players head for the courts, and bikini-clad sun seekers lie down on their brightly colored beach towels for a serious tanning session.

Exercise 5B
1. Yes 2. remove comma 3. insert two commas 4. Yes 5. Yes

Exercise 6A
Most experts agree, despite conclusive evidence, that the lemon tree probably originated in southeast Asia in the vicinity of Burma thousands of years ago. Although this evergreen tree is sensitive to freezing weather, the fruit does best, as a matter of fact, exposed to the occasional cold snap that a hot, humid climate lacks. California growers, as a result, use wind machines and heaters in their groves to regulate temperature. Lemon trees, under ideal conditions, can bear buds, flowers, developing fruit, and mature fruit all at the same time. Citrus trees, moreover, require a fair amount of water; rain, however, can damage the fruit. Every part of the fruit, we are told, from seed to peel has a use from food preparation and general household use to medicinal and commercial applications. Most of us, without a doubt, use lemons most frequently as flavor intensifiers. In some cultures people, indeed, know the meaning of using the entire fruit: they eat the lemon as we would an apple, peel and all.

Exercise 6B
1. remove both commas 2. Yes 3. insert comma after <u>men</u> 4. Yes 5. insert two commas

Exercise 7A
1. "I don't entirely agree, Jim, with your position," said Ella.
2. "Ella, you never agree with me," said Jim.
3. "I agree with you most of the time, Jim," said Ella.
4. "Well then, Ella, why don't you agree with me now?" said Jim.
5. "Jim, I cannot agree with you because you are wrong," said Ella.
6. "Ella, tell me that you love me anyway," said Jim.

Exercise 7B
1. No 2. No 3. No 4. Yes 5. No
1. Scott, 2. manager, Mrs. 3. requested, sir, 4. correct 5. you, one and all,

Exercise 8A
1. My friend Carla Caraway went to New York to get a job as a dancer. (No commas needed.)
2. A young woman, alone in a strange city, must learn how to take care of herself.
3. She auditioned for Judith Jamison, the famous choreographer of the Alvin Ailey company.
4. Carla, breathless and exhausted, waited after the audition to hear the choreographer's opinion.
5. Carla joined the Ailey company, one of the best dance companies in the world.

Exercise 8B
1. The talented American contralto, Marian Anderson, who had sung at the White House, was barred from singing in Constitution Hall in Washington.
2. Instead, Ms. Anderson sang at the Lincoln Memorial before 75,000 people who had gathered in support of her. (comma optional)
3. Three Aaron Copland ballets, drawing upon American themes, are *Billy the Kid, Rodeo,* and *Appalachian Spring.*
4. Copland wrote *Appalachian Spring* for Martha Graham, choreographer and dancer.
5. Ernest Hemingway, an American author, began his first job as a newspaper reporter at the age of eighteen.
6. no commas
7. no commas
8. Gilbert Stuart, an early American painter, is best known for his portraits of George Washington.

9. Frank Lloyd Wright, one of the first architects to use glass and metal walls for office buildings, achieved early recognition outside the United States.
10. no commas

Exercise 9A
1. "I can never do these homework **assignments**," Gary complained.
2. "**Well,**" said his **mother,** "you haven't even tried."
3. "I never learn anything in that class**," he said,** "so what's the point?"
4. "**Besides,**" he said to **her,** "I have a date tonight."
5. "**Gary,** you should do your assignment before you go **out,**" his mother advised.
6. "I have to leave in one **hour,**" he told his mother.
7. "If you begin to work right no**w,**" she **said,** "you will have plenty of time."
8. "I'll do it when I **return,**" he said as he left the house.
9. "**Gary,** come right back **here,**" she **called,** "and finish your homework."
10. "You might as well **relax, Mom,**" said Gary's sister. "He has already gone."

Exercise 9B
1. "**Greg,** did you hear about the recent triathalon competition in Hawaii?" Diane asked.
2. "I hadn't **realized,**" she **continued,** "how popular the sport has become."
3. "The athlete who attempts the Ironman competition must be in top physical **condition, Diane,**" Greg replied.
4. "Most other triathalon competitions, **as a matter of fact,** are not as demanding as the **Ironman,**" he pointed out.
5. "If your **goal,** Greg, is just to complete the **triathalon,**" Diane **said,** "you don't need to worry about speed."
6. The doctor **said,** "Hypothermia can be a threat to the swimmers if the water is especially cold."
7. "One of the greatest dangers to the athletes during the marathon **run," he added,** "is dehydration."
8. "For most **triathalons,** competitors are required to sign waivers releasing the promoters from responsibility for the athletes' **safety,**" Greg said.
9. Diane **remarked,** "The most successful athletes, **as I might have expected,** train under conditions similar to those of the competition."
10. "Competitors should train for at least three **months," the doctor advised,** "in each of the three sports: **swimming, running, and cycling.**"

Exercise 10A
1. George will move to Las Vegas, Nevada, in January.
2. His address has been The Stanford Arms Hotel, 536 W. 18th Street, Rittman, Indiana 46206, for the last six years.
3. We will forward his mail to his new address: The Luxor Hotel, Las Vegas, Nevada 89501.
4. Bill Wilson is a salesperson for Fashion Clothing Co., 2473 White Plains Road, Bronx, New York 10111.
5. On 15 April 2005, Bill traveled from New York to Dallas, Texas, to attend a fashion show.
6. The fashion show was held at the Plaza Hotel, 8 Fifth Street, Dallas, Texas.

Exercise 10B
1. No 2. Yes 3. Yes 4. Yes 5. No 6. No
1. Send Lynn's mail in care of Mrs. R. B. Singer, 1532 Stone Canyon Drive, Santa Maria, Arizona 85321, starting Tuesday, July 19, 2005.

5. Nat wrote to the American Association of Community Colleges at One Dupont Circle, Washington, D.C. 20036, for a list of colleges in Texas and Arizona.

6. Charles Lindbergh, flying the "Spirit of Saint Louis," left Mineola, New York, on May 20, 1927, and arrived in Paris, France, on May 21, 1927.

Group Activity   Answers will vary.

Lesson 11 Suggested Sentences

A. The 100-inch Hooker telescope at Mount Wilson, California, built in 1917, helped produce some of the triumphs of 20th-century astronomy, including the Big Bang theory.

B. Although the 100-inch telescope was considered obsolete in 1985, new inventions and a determined effort by a group of rich private benefactors saved the Hooker from oblivion and reopened the historic telescope in 1994.

C. Although tree-ripened lemons have more flavor, most lemons are picked green and put into storage for later shipment to supermarkets across the country.

D. Rollerbladers who start at the art museum head north along the east bank of the river on the smooth, flat, level pavement, which runs for miles and is ideal for both beginning and speed skaters.

Chapter Summary

1. main 2. series, three 3. phrase 4. subordinate 5. two 6. interrupts 7. set off 8. nonessential
9. direct 10. item

Practice Test

I. 1. The senator, in the meantime, …

2. No commas

3. No commas

4. helmet, jacket, jeans, and

5. While painting, the women…

6. ... bag, which… seat, ….

7. No commas

8. team, but

9. Wall Street, a narrow street in lower Manhattan, is one of the world's great financial districts.

10. Readers, would you....

11. No commas

12. No commas

13. ... affordability, " Senator Bidwell asserted, "is a national issue."

14. down, people

15. ... a bicycle, a surfboard, a camera, or a radio with his prize money.

16. ... The Nature Conservancy, 4245 N. Fairfax Drive, Suite 100, Arlington, VA 22203-1606,
last week.

17. To protect her photographs, Chiara

18. No commas

19. No commas

20. gentle, wavy

II. Answers will vary.

Editing Practice

Last summer Juan Romero, a schoolteacher, and his family drove across the country from Pueblo, Colorado, to Washington, D.C. They left Pueblo on July 2 in their new, brown, tightly-packed mini van, and they planned to return on August 31. Since they were going to be away a long time, Mr. Romero had asked the post office to forward their mail to them at their friends' house, 22654 Constitution Drive, Washington, D.C. After leaving Pueblo, Mr. Romero and his wife, Julia, and their four children, Alfredo, Maria, Pedro, and Juan Jr., drove south to Santa Fe, New Mexico. As the Romeros drove east along Route 40, they passed an Indian trading post. "Let's stop here," Alfredo shouted. When the car rolled to a stop, Mr. and Mrs. Romero gave each child some money to spend in the trading post. In a short while, they returned to the car carrying Indian arrowheads, peace pipes, pottery, and a feather headdress. The family, who were now even more crowded together in the car, drove through Texas, Arkansas, and Tennessee. Mrs. Romero could tell that the children were bored, so she persuaded her husband to stop in Memphis at Graceland. In a flash, the four youngsters escaped from the back seat to buy autographed records, a large plastic guitar, a harmonica, and a white cowboy hat. Once back on the road, Mr. Romero said he would not stop again until they reached their destination. However, before they traveled much farther, they had made several stops at parrot jungles, alligator farms, and other roadside attractions, even stopping at the beach in Norfolk, Virginia. "On our trip back to Colorado," said Mrs. Romero, "we'll have no room to sit if we stop at one more place." From then on, therefore, they just bought food, which filled their stomachs but not the car. After seeing the sights in Washington, D.C., they returned to Pueblo, and the whole family agreed that they had had a memorable vacation.

Chapter 9

Usage
Lesson 1

Exercise 1A   Sentences will vary in this exercise and in the second part of each exercise throughout.

Exercise 1B 1. accept 2. except

Exercise 1C 1. advise 2. advice

Exercise 1D 1. affect 2. effect

Exercise 1E 1. all ready 2. already

Mini Review 1 1. effect, advice 2. all ready, except 3. except, an
4. already, affected 5. advise, accept

Lesson 2

Exercise 2A 1. dessert 2. desert 3. deserted

Exercise 2B 1. It's 2. its

Exercise 2C 1. no 2. knows

Exercise 2D 1. lead 2. led

Exercise 2E 1. lose 2. loose

Mini Review 2 1. led, desert 2. know, desserts 3. no, lead 4. led, its 5. it's, loose 6. know, lose, deserts

Lesson 3

Exercise 3A 1. past 2. passed

Exercise 3B 1. personal 2. personnel

Exercise 3C 1. principles 2. principal

Exercise 3D 1. quiet 2. quite, quiet

Exercise 3E 1. supposed 2. suppose

Exercise 3F 1. than 2. then

Exercise 3G 1. There 2. they're, their

Mini Review 3 1. principles, personal 2. supposed, than 3. quite, personnel 4. past, supposed 5. They're, than

Lesson 4

Exercise 4A 1. Though 2. thought, through

Exercise 4B 1. two 2. too, to

Exercise 4C 1. used 2. used

Exercise 4D 1. weather 2. whether

Exercise 4E 1. Who's 2. whose

Exercise 4F 1. You're 2. your

Mini Review 4 1. Who's, your 2. thought, used 3. whether, your, weather 4. Whose, two 5. too, who's

Group Activity
know, there, losing, It's, too, principal, a, personnel, quite, They're, where, an, led, than, accepting, effect, advise, supposed, their

Punctuation
Exercise 1A
Pictographs, ancient painting on rock surfaces, have fascinated people for many years. Who created these paintings? Why did they paint on the surfaces of rocks and caves? It is generally believed that the ancestors of modern Native American tribes produced these paintings as answers for spiritual needs. Indian artists used two methods of drawing on stone. The first involved engraving the surface of rocks, resulting in designs known as petroglyphs. The second and more common method involved painting with colored minerals on the surface of the rocks. These are pictographs. Does anyone know exactly how long ago these rock paintings were made?

Exercise 2A
1. kachinas; these 2. Claus; in 3. kachinas; they 4. mammals: rooster 5. water: lightning
6. objects; they

Group Activity
Mrs. Stephanie Culp
Priority Management Systems, Inc.
1379 Heather Lane
Baltimore, MD 21203

Dear Mrs. **Culp:**
I recently read an article that explained how your company, Priority Management Systems, **Inc.,** helps make business offices more **efficient.** I would like your advice about the following **problems:** I have a messy desk, an overflowing file cabinet, and a drawer full of unpaid **bills.** The article stated that you advise executives as **follows:** set up a system of baskets on the desk to sort out the **papers;** however, I can never find the time to stop and rearrange my **papers.** Would you be willing to visit my office to help me get **organized?** I would be very **appreciative; furthermore,** I would be willing to pay you well for your **time.**
Please send me a copy of your book, *How to Get Organized When You Don't Have the Time,* as soon as **possible.**
Sincerely yours,
Annette Harris

Exercise 3A
1. "Have you ever watched *TV Mystery Theater* ?" he asked.
2. no quotation marks
3. "I'll pay for lunch tomorrow if we win tonight"?
4. "When I was three years old," Rose said, "my favorite poem was *The Owl and the Pussycat.*"
5. "I am resigning at the end of this month";

Exercise 3B Sentences will vary.

Sentence Mechanics
Exercise 1A
1. President Abraham Lincoln 2. Kentucky 3. winter, February 4. Presidents' Day 5. Whig 6. Civil War 7. The Gettysburg Address, Gettysburg, Pennsylvania 8. The Emancipation Proclamation 9. John Wilkes Booth 10. Ford's Theater in Washington, D.C. 11. Oak Ridge

Cemetery, Springfield, Illinois 12. Potomac 13. American History 14. The White House, 1600 Pennsylvania Avenue, Washington, D.C.

Exercise 1B
1. Ann Nguyen, American
2. I'm, English 1, I'm, History 21
3. When Mary, New York, Metropolitan Museum of Art
4. I, *Phantom of the Opera*
5. Sue's, Ritz, Kraft, Coca-Cola
6. When Darlene, Sears, Wamsutta
7. Are, Sugar Bowl, New Year's Day
8. In, I, Saturdays
9. Yellowstone National Park, United States
10. My, Hemingway, I

Exercise 1C
1. My son brushes with Crest toothpaste every morning.
2. We visited the Liberty Bell in Philadelphia last August.
3. I don't think that the senator should have traveled at government expense to the French Riviera, do you?
4. Paul likes to watch *Good Morning America* every morning before going to work at Boeing Aircraft Co.
5. Chuck said, "Let's go to a rock concert next Saturday."

Exercise 2A
1. CIA 2. U.S. Navy 3. Dr. 4. OSU 5. Derryk B. Jones, Jr. 6. Ms. A.M.

Exercise 3A
1. <u>48</u> forty-eight 2. <u>eight percent</u> 8 percent 3. <u>nine grams</u> 9 grams 4. C 5. <u>50 years</u> fifty 6. C
7. <u>seventy-two, seventy</u> 72, 70 8. <u>Ten</u> 10 9. C 10. <u>four thousand two-hundred feet</u> 4,200

Lesson 4 Suggested Sentences
A. Mr. Furutani, who translates foreign languages for a worldwide translating company, enjoys working from his home.
B. The Native American artists, whose paintings have been found in caves, used abstract symbols that may represent the visions or dreams of the artists.
C. Lightweight radios and tape units equipped with tiny headphones, the nation's latest electronic fad, entertain joggers and automobile drivers.
D. The Argentine Gaucho, a cowboy of the pampas, uses the bola, a rope
with weights attached, to catch cattle or game by entangling their legs.

Chapter Summary
1. period 2. question mark 3. semicolon 4. colon 5. quotation marks
6. comma 7. capital

Practice Test
I. 1. ... advertisement.
2. .....staff.
3. crash?

4. Hooray! heard!
5. ... September 30.

II. 1. Chicago has . . .library; however,....
2. locations: New York; Texas; Oregon;
3. hike:
4. 11:30 ... paper; the essay was due at 8:00 the next morning.
5. eyes;

III. 1. The Jordans ... Dallas Cowboys
2. Last spring I ... South ... Texas to Florida.
3. Dale ... Spanish ... Adams Community College.
4. My Aunt Sophie's ... Fritos.
5. On Tuesday ... Oval Office.

IV. 1. M.D. 2. IRS 3. MN 4. $65.78 5. NYU

V. 1. Four 2. 40 boxes 15 boxes 3. three hours two suitcases 4. pages 15 through 21 Chapter 8
5. $79.50 $4.25

VI. Sentences will vary.

Editing Practice

         museum   **New York City**
A remarkable <u>M</u>useum has opened its doors in <u>NYC</u>. It is the Rose Center for Earth and Space at

    American Museum of Natural History Two hundred ten
the <u>a</u>merican <u>m</u>useum of <u>n</u>atural <u>h</u>istory. <u>$210</u>-million was spent to make this building the world's

        planetarium
most advanced <u>P</u>lanetarium. Visitors can learn about star clusters, gas clouds, and galaxies, with
              NASA   **eight**
all the information coming from <u>N.A.S.A</u>. The visitors stand atop an <u>8</u>-foot deep bowl to
              After
view light and laser effects. <u>a</u>fter the show, visitors exit onto a long runway that circles the
                                Asia Europe
sphere's exterior. "The Rose Space Center will bring in visitors from <u>a</u>sia, <u>e</u>urope, and
Africa   **Dr.** **V.**
<u>a</u>frica to learn about their universe," D<u>r</u> Ellen <u>V</u> Futter, the museum's president, claims. Dr.
       president   **thirteen**
Futter had been <u>P</u>resident at Barnard College in Manhattan for <u>13</u> years before coming to the

 museum. She is delighted that the Rose Space Center will draw visitors with varying educational

        college
backgrounds, unlike a <u>C</u>ollege with strict admission standards.

Chapter 10
Exercise 2A Suggested Topic Sentences
A. My experiences at the college bookstore were truly disagreeable. (or unpleasant)
B. Fish have developed various ways of communicating with each other.
C. The gold miners of the 1850s faced daily hardships, but few became rich men in spite of their efforts.
D. The life of Albert Einstein was full of hardships as well as rewards.
E. All too many Americans, who would not regard themselves as drug addicts, are dependent on drugs.

Exercise 3A
A. Cross out the following sentences: 2 and 5. B. Cross out sentences 2 and 4. C. Cross out sentences 1 and 4. D. Cross out sentences 2 and 6.
Student sentences will vary.

Exercise 3B
Cross out the following sentences: My physics class never reviewed any subject we had already studied. The teacher expected us to know everything. My math teacher ignored the textbook he had assigned and just lectured during class time. My teachers in other classes made the tests too hard by not telling us what would be on them. I was discouraged by my low grades.
Student sentences will vary.

Exercise 4B Suggested Answers
1. However 2. In fact 3. First, Second, Third, Fourth 4. for example 5. for instance, In addition, on the other hand 6. moreover, Consequently 7. in contrast

Exercise 4C
Pre-Columbian Mexican art was collected extensively by the famous artist Diego Rivera. His collection of ceramic figures resulted in the first exhibit of the art of Western Mexico in 1946 in Mexico City. Since <u>then</u>, many exhibitions of these figures have been organized all over the world. <u>Now</u>, we recognize that West Mexican art consists mainly of ceramic figure sculpture that was found in tombs in the present Mexican states of Nayarit, Jalisco, and Colima. <u>However</u>, today these three names are used to describe pottery based on style rather than geography. It is clear, <u>for example</u>, that typical Nayarit figures can occur in the same tombs with figures of the Jalisco type. These artists of West Mexico made both large hollow and small solid tomb figures. Both have been found in the same burial chamber. <u>To illustrate</u>, the figures of Nayarit are characterized by their active forms, with clearly defined fingers and toes. Arms were usually long, thin ropes of clay. No attention was paid to anatomical details of the arms. <u>Moreover</u>, in the Nayarit figures, great attention was paid to the hair, which was incised in many straight lines. Figures of both sexes wore round earrings, nose ornaments, and facial markings that look like long slashes on the cheeks. <u>Furthermore</u>, these figures were usually painted red. <u>On the other hand</u>, Jalisco figures were usually gray or cream colored. The heads of the Jalisco figures were elongated and decorated with an ornament that crisscrosses the head. <u>In addition</u>, they had enlarged, staring eyes, hatchet-shaped noses, and large, open mouths, with the teeth clearly defined. <u>In contrast</u>, the Colima figures were usually bright orange to deep red with spots of black scattered over their surface. The human figures of the Colima group were posed in a stiffly mannered style. It looks as though they were posing for the artist. No form of engraving or other decoration was used. The Colima figures were often animals, especially dogs. These dogs are thought to have been the gods that escorted the humans to the next world. <u>In conclusion</u>, these clay figures are only a small part of the artistic output of the

ancient Mexican people. We can never know about their music, their oral literature, their wood sculpture or their textiles. But the clay sculptures are beautiful works done by master artists.

Appendix Editing Practice
Sentences

Exercise 1
1. mens' men's 2. forgave forgiven 3. There's There are 4. myself me 5. Set Sit 6. studying Ed studying, Ed 7. show shows 8. following; following: 9. working, and working and 10. work however work; however,

Exercise 2
1. will choose would choose 2. more high higher 3. Aunt aunt 4. noon, we noon; we 5. If Rachel leads the discussion. Everyone If Rachel leads the discussion, everyone 6. work as a rule work, as a rule, 7. one hundred eighty-six 186 8. I me 9. looks look 10. theres there's

Exercise 3
1. Community College community college 2. ripe. ripe? 3. more better better 4. goals; goals: 5. it Adina broke the plate when she dropped a glass on it. 6. While you were sleeping. While you were sleeping, 7. This Teaching is a rewarding occupation. 8. tonight" tonight," 9. Who's Whose 10. Shapiro however Shapiro, however,

Exercise 4
1. him he 2. a hard worker hard working 3. it's its 4. June 17, 2001 June 17, 2001, 5. most fastest the fastest 6. seem seems 7. has auditioned had auditioned 8. Ave Avenue 9. The essay easy for Brad to write. The essay was easy for Brad to write; he was glad 10. There's There are

Exercise 5
1. dutys duties 2. I me 3. more faster faster 4. key, keys; 5. the letter the letter, 6. their its 7. excited, when excited when 8. mississippi river Mississippi River 9. that is who are 10. testses tests

Exercise 6
1. had traveled will have traveled 2. fathers father's 3. on the map. You on the map, you 4. except accept 5. Admissions Office but Admissions Office, but 6. most softest softest 7. Here's Here are 8. film nevertheless she film; nevertheless, she 9. he Rudy said to Alberto, "I owe Martin fifty dollars." (or) Rudy, who owed Martin fifty dollars, told Alberto about his debt. 10. myself I

Exercise 7
1. has gave has given 2. May, and May and 3. cheerleader, who cheerleader who 4. show shows 5. Washington D.C. Washington, D.C. 6. was riding were riding 7. sport. You sport. I 8. a an 9. to too 10. photoes photos

Exercise 8
1. tuition, he tuition; however, he 2. washing the car with her collie walked by with her collie 3. use used 4. carefully Mario carefully, Mario 5. are required is required 6. So many students drinking coffee between classes The cafeteria was crowded today because so many

students were drinking coffee between classes. 7. <u>has been laying</u> has been lying 8. <u>knows</u> has known 9. <u>Who's</u> Whose 10. <u>their</u> its

Exercise 9
1. <u>Whose</u> Who's 2. <u>have promise</u> have promised 3. <u>me</u> I 4. <u>you're</u> your 5. <u>day-care centers,</u> day-care centers; 6. <u>Tim's job; furthermore,</u> Tim's job, furthermore, 7. <u>There's</u> There are 8. <u>calculator and</u> calculator, and 9. <u>effected</u> affected 10. <u>is laying</u> is lying

Exercise 10
1. <u>have</u> has 2. <u>loafs</u> loaves 3. <u>her's</u> hers 4. <u>Writing hundreds of letters</u> By writing hundreds of letters, the voters turned public opinion against the project. 5. <u>are</u> is 6. <u>their</u> her 7. <u>Edison . . .inventor</u> Edison, who was a famous American inventor, is 8. <u>Justin asking if I would meet him for lunch.</u> Justin asked if I would meet him for lunch, but I had promised to go shopping with Val. 9. <u>The film won four awards,</u> The film won four awards; it 10. <u>that "he ...tip."</u> that he always...tip.

Paragraphs

I. The New York Botanical Garden's forest stands in the Bronx. We usually associate the Bronx with the Yankees and urban blight, but we would never think of a fifty- acre forest. The wooded land contains one of New York's treasures. "Most people don't even know about it," said Ken Lauby, the Botanical Garden's vice president. "Most people who come to the Garden want to see the flowers. We would love for more people to see and appreciate the forest," he added. It's a tough time to be a tree. New York and other cities are struggling to find money for the forest. Trees can't talk at City Council meetings, so if money has to be cut, it's usually the money for the Botanical Garden. But did you know that one hundred trees remove about a ton of pollution from the air each year? After a highway was built nearby, some trees close to the roadway started to grow more slowly. The forest faces other urban pressures. Its soil contains high concentrations of heavy metals; therefore, water penetrates at a slower rate than normal. Also, because visitors have tramped down the earth on some trails, new plants haven't been able to grow. But the woods have managed to thrive despite the stress.

II. Although there is now an association of devoted boomerang throwers, the boomerang is not likely to have a noticeable effect on American sports. Companies that manufacture golf clubs and tennis rackets shouldn't be alarmed. The flat, curved wooden boomerang served Australian aborigine tribes as a battle weapon and as a hunting weapon for small animals, birds, and fish. When this device is hurled, it returns to the hand of the thrower; however, the thrower must be an expert. Today it's made of glass, laminated birch, polymer fiber, and other materials. Called "the thinking man's Frisbee," its appeal is mostly to men such as engineers and pilots. There are approximately twenty U.S. tournaments each year and a World Cup event every two years for enthusiasts. A champion can throw a boomerang as far as the length of a football field and at the speed of over sixty miles an hour. Collectors range from the Smithsonian Institute in our nation's capital to a man in Canton, Ohio, with 15,000 boomerangs in his private collection.

III. Hungry, ugly, giant lizards have invaded some towns in southern Florida. They are iguanas that had once been kept as pets, but they are now rapidly reproducing in the wild. The manager of a condominium said, "Iguanas eat the flowers, mess up the pools, and dirty the sidewalks and lawns." Most of the time, iguanas like to lie in the grass in the warm sunshine, and they hide in the treetops or in holes they have dug in the ground. An iguana can grow up to six feet in length, and its weight can be up to thirteen pounds. Some iguanas are larger than any lizard found naturally in the United States. They have fiercer tempers than many of the ancient dinosaurs. In theory, a good, long cold snap should kill the iguanas, but they have learned that if they stayed in water, they had a better chance of keeping warm. Since iguanas are excellent swimmers, they can stay submerged for fifteen minutes. At one point, the residents of some towns in Florida hired a trapper, but the lizards ran really fast and managed to escape her traps. One man said, "It's impossible to capture them; they are too smart for that." There's little doubt that if you met an iguana in an alley or in your pool, you would be pretty scared.

IV. Every summer wild fires in our forests burn millions of acres of trees, posing a threat to everything in their path. An elite group, known as the Arrowhead Hotshots, stands ready at two hours' notice to take on one of the riskiest assignments a firefighter can face. The Hotshots are sent to the most hazardous situations; they go where the terrain, fire behavior, and fuel make the fire most dangerous to fight. Founded in 1981, the organization's work center is located at an elevation of 6240 feet in the General Grant district of Kings Canyon National Park in California. The candidates who arrive to enter the strenuous training program must be in top physical condition, for the highly structured exercises will call upon all their strength and endurance. When they are fighting a fire, a typical shift can last sixteen hours under conditions that are physically exhausting and emotionally draining. Since they must live and work together as a unit for approximately six months, the program stresses compatibility and team spirit. Over the years, tools and equipment have been really improved, but the crew working on the ground is indispensable in finally putting out the flames.

V. In spring of 1915, a five-piece band of white musicians from New Orleans opened in a café in an African-American neighborhood of Chicago. Jazz was beginning to find an audience among blacks but was unfamiliar to most white patrons. The band was not an immediate success, but after a lot of persuading, people started coming to dance at the cafe. By the time Louis Armstrong arrived in 1922, however, the scene had changed. As a part of the "Great Migration," which began after World War I, Armstrong recalled, "There was plenty of work, lots of Dough flying around, all kinds of beautiful women at your service." He added that a musician at the time was treated like a god. By the end of the 20's, over a million black people from the Deep South had settled in Chicago's South Side. They worked in the stockyards, in the steel mills, on the railroads, and in heavy industry. There were clubs for blacks only, but there were also those known as "black and tans" where both races mingled. The black musicians from the South felt at home in Chicago, and white musicians were attracted to their music. Despite the alarmists who predicted that such crude sounds would corrupt the morals of young people, jazz flourished in Chicago. This was still a segregated world, but black and white musicians liked to get together and to play in clubs on the South Side after closing hours. By 1928, the scene changed again, and many of the musicians who were no longer able to make a living in Chicago went to New York. Nevertheless, those early years in Chicago brought a wider audience to jazz than the dancers who had swung to the music on the South Side at the beginning of the decade.

VI. What picture comes to your mind's eye when you hear the word "hula"? If you are like most of us, you see the following Hollywood stereotype: a lovely young woman wearing a cellophane version of a grass skirt, seductively rolling and swaying her hips to the strumming of a ukulele. The hula hoop, used for exercise and play, has taken its name from this popular image; one must move the hips in a gyrating motion to keep the hoop spinning. According to the many Hawaiians now living on the mainland, people in over thirty states are dancing the hula. Although many of these dancers are creating their own experimental versions of the dance, they remain in touch with the ancient traditions. They want, however, to eliminate Hollywood's interpretation of the hula. The significance of the dance, they maintain, is not in the movement of hands and hips, but in the chants that preserve the legends and history of the Hawaiian people. Passed down from teacher to student, the hula survived a fifty-year ban by missionaries, a long period of neglect, and the glitz of the movies. Despite the innovations of today's dancers, it seems likely that these ancient ceremonies will last for another century or two.

VII. The ranchers of frontier days admired the wild horses roaming the range lands of the West for their stamina and speed. They even captured some of the finest mustangs to breed with their horses. But as farm machinery came into common use, the horse no longer played a vital role in ranching and farming. Wild horses began to be regarded as a nuisance. Ranchers didn't want mustangs sharing the range with their ever-increasing herds of cattle. Today the residents of the Southwest are divided by what some call "The Mustang Dilemma." People are debating the question of how many are too many. But are they talking about horses or people? Reno, Nevada, one of the most rapidly growing cities of the West, is a good example of people invading the mustang's range. The wild horses already now graze at the edges of the suburbs amidst power lines, walls, fences, traffic, and mile after mile of paved highways.
On one side of the controversy are those who want fewer cattle on the range and more protection and room for the mustang. On the other side, in addition to the ranchers' concerns, some people want to protect the habitat of wild life in the area. They argue that herds must be thinned periodically, or they pose a threat not only to all wild life, but to mustangs themselves as they compete for the range land that is left. Both sides make convincing arguments, but on behalf of the mustang, consider this fact: it has given its name to a WWII aircraft, a motorcycle seat, a football team, and a very popular car. Like those early ranchers, we also admire the mustang.

VIII. Yoga classes offer a unique opportunity to refine your yoga practice through repatterning mind-body functioning. By observing closely what is going on in your body, your instructor will tailor each session to your individual needs. You will be well advised to wear loosely fitting clothing and to bring a sticky mat to lie on. With her hands-on guidance, you will learn healthful movement patterns, relieve the stress in chronic pain areas, and expand your range of motion while increasing strength and flexibility. Her one-on-one approach will deepen your experience of the yoga poses and provide a sequence of poses that address your particular needs. Receive deep-tissue bodywork, assisted stretches, and adjustments while in the yoga poses.
The classes target the following conditions: chronic back, neck, and shoulder pain; joint problems; arthritic conditions; traumatic injuries; post-surgery rehabilitation; illness recovery.
Your instructor's years of yoga, movement and bodywork experience provide a safe and deeply caring environment. She is a Registered Movement Therapist, Registered Somatic Movement Educator and Certified Practitioner of Body-Mind Centering (BMC), based on the work of teacher, healer and Somatic Bodywork pioneer Bonnie Bainbridge-Cohen. Her dedication to yoga is shaped by her lifetime as a performance and visual artist, dancer, and movement researcher. She has studied many therapeutic modalities including Shiatsu, Rolfing, Feldenkrais, and Pilates.

REPRODUCIBLE MATERIALS

The following pages contain three Chapter Tests for each chapter in *Sentence Dynamics,* a Midterm Exam, and a Final Exam. You are hereby granted permission to photocopy the individual pages that follow for classroom use.

Chapter 1 Test: Nouns and Pronouns
Form A

Name _____

Date _____ Class Time _____

Instructor _____

I. Using the noun test and your dictionary, identify each word as a noun or some other part of a sentence. If the word is a noun, place a check under the column headed Noun. If it is not a noun, place a check under the column headed Other. (20 points, 2 points each)

	Noun	Other
1. sincerely	_____	_____
2. decimal	_____	_____
3. computer	_____	_____
4. that	_____	_____
5. between	_____	_____
6. July	_____	_____
7. together	_____	_____
8. seen	_____	_____
9. triangle	_____	_____
10. runner	_____	_____

II. Write N above each common or proper noun. Use the noun test and your dictionary. (15 points, 3 points each)

1. Gina had no change to put in the meter.

2. Did Jim see the Celtics play at Boston Garden on Friday?

3. Sofi has lived in three countries in Europe.

4. When Mr. Palka graduated, his dream became a reality.

5. Trash piled up in the streets during the strike.

III. Each of the following sentences contains an error in the possessive form of a noun. Underline each error. Then write the correct form on the line at the right. (5 points, 1 point each)

1. The children's fifth-grade teacher took the students to the museum.   _____
2. Doris has a years lease on the apartment.   _____
3. The first-graders Halloween drawings decorated the walls of their classroom.   _____
4. The chairs in a dentists office should be comfortable.   _____
5. "Dilbert" by Scott Adams is Julius favorite comic strip.   _____

IV. Change the underlined nouns to the possessive form. Write the possessive form on the line at the right. (10 points, 2 points each)

1. the notes that belong to the <u>speaker</u>   _____
2. the compliments of several <u>customers</u>   _____

3. the career of my <u>father-in-law</u>   _____
4. the plans of the <u>family</u>   _____
5. the athletic club that belongs to the <u>women</u>   _____

V. Each of the following sentences contains a shift in a personal pronoun. Identify each error by drawing a line under the incorrect pronoun. Write the correct form on the line at the right. (10 points, 2 points each)

1. When George becomes acquainted with a customer, he will do special favors for
them.   _____
2. The coach told us that you must show up for practice.   _____
3. Whenever Sara greets her guests, she really makes you feel at home.   _____
4. Any motorist who runs a red light is a dangerous driver. They can cause fatal
accidents.   _____
5. If a person wants to attend the Rose Parade, they should plan to camp out
the night before on Colorado Blvd.   _____

VI. Correct the spelling errors in the underlined pronoun forms. (10 points, 2 points each)

1. The dog has lost <u>it's</u> collar.   _____
2. <u>You're</u> library card has expired.   _____
3. I forgot my counseling appointment, but Mel and Takeo remembered <u>theirs'</u>.   _____
4. Since you didn't bring your lunch, please have some of <u>our's</u>.   _____
5. <u>Who's</u> turn is it to deal the cards?   _____

VII. Write <u>two</u> sentences using the possessive form of <u>singular</u> nouns. Write <u>three</u> sentences using the possessive form of <u>plural</u> nouns. (15 points, 3 points each)

1. _____

2. _____

3. _____

4. _____

5. _____

VIII. Write the plural forms of the following nouns. (10 points, 2 points each)

1. hero _____
2. fox _____
3. witch _____
4. mouse _____
5. bounty _____

45

IX. If the use of the underlined pronoun is correct, write C on the line. If the use of the pronoun is incorrect, write the correct pronoun on the line. (5 points, 1 point each)

1. My sister and <u>myself</u> were born in Cuba. _____

2. At the end of the campaign, they congratulated <u>theirselves.</u> _____

3. Deshaun watched <u>hisself</u> dance in the studio mirror. _____

4. We could hardly recognize <u>ourselfs</u> in the picture. _____

5. She treated <u>herself</u> to a haircut in an expensive salon. _____

Chapter 1 Test: Nouns and Pronouns
Form B

Name _____

Date _____ Class Time _____

Instructor _____

I. Using the noun test and your dictionary, identify each word as a noun or some other part of a sentence. If the word is a noun, place a check under the column headed Noun. If it is not a noun, place a check under the column headed Other. (20 points, 2 points each)

	Noun	**Other**
1. cheesecake	_____	_____
2. pastime	_____	_____
3. though	_____	_____
4. where	_____	_____
5. trials	_____	_____
6. Houston	_____	_____
7. waited	_____	_____
8. harsh	_____	_____
9. department	_____	_____
10. lose	_____	_____

II. Write N above each common or proper noun. Use the noun test and your dictionary. (15 points, 3 points each)

1. The recent disaster tested the courage of the volunteers.
2. Andy's sister works in the drugstore during the summer.
3. Like many students, Lisa has a part-time job.
4. The driver opened the trunk and took out the spare tire.
5. Mr. Evans taped a notice on the classroom door.

III. Each of the following sentences contains an error in the possessive form of a noun. Underline the error. Then write the correct form on the line at the right. (5 points, 1 point each)

1. The governors husband manufactures hardware for computers.   _____
2. She washed her mothers car.   _____
3. Mr. Smiths report eventually led to an investigation.   _____
4. The coachs voice rose as he lectured the team.   _____
5. The womans face was caked with makeup.   _____

IV. Change the underlined nouns to the possessive form. Write the possessive form on the line at the right. (10 points, 2 points each)

1. the eyes of the two babies   _____
2. the husband of Mrs. Marcus   _____
3. the parents of Marian   _____
4. a delay of three weeks   _____
5. the jackets that belong to the men   _____

47

V. Each of the following sentences contains a shift in a personal pronoun. Identify each error by drawing a line under the incorrect pronoun. Write the correct form on the line at the right. (10 points, 2 points each)

1. Julie carries an extra pen in her purse because you never know when a pen might run out of ink.   _____

2. I shouldn't have eaten those two candy bars. It will probably spoil my appetite for lunch.   _____

3. Even when a customer is very demanding, Kim is always polite to them.   _____

4. Jason likes to read books that you can finish in an hour or so.   _____

5. If a person owns a boat, they should know how to swim.   _____

VI. Correct the spelling errors in the underlined pronoun forms. (10 points, 2 points each)

1. Our dog offers it's paw to everyone.   _____

2. Who's keys are these?   _____

3. I no longer believe you're promises.   _____

4. You saw Glen's photos of Yosemite, but you haven't seen ours'.   _____

5. We brought our lunches, but they did not bring theirs'.   _____

VII. Write two sentences using the possessive form of singular nouns. Write three sentences using the possessive form of plural nouns. (15 points, 3 points each)

1. _____

2. _____

3. _____

4. _____

5. _____

VIII. Write the plural forms of the following nouns. (10 points, 2 points each)

1. loss _____
2. wife _____
3. leaf _____
4. veto _____
5. party _____

IX. If the use of the underlined pronoun is correct, write C on the line. If the use of the pronoun is incorrect, write the correct pronoun on the line. (5 points, 1 point each)

1. The restaurant owner himself recommended the wine.   _____

2. The news about Ron surprised Lauren and myself.   _____

3. They spent Sunday quietly by theirselves.   _____

4. She reminded herself to be on time.   _____

5. We entertained ourself by playing computer games.   _____

Chapter 1 Test: Nouns and Pronouns
Form C

Name _____
Date _____ Class Time _____
Instructor _____

I. Using the noun test and your dictionary, identify each word as a noun or some other part of sentence. If the word is a noun, place a check under the column headed Noun. If it is not a noun, place a check under the column headed Other. (20 points, 2 points each)

	Noun	**Other**
1. agreement	_____	_____
2. liquid	_____	_____
3. new	_____	_____
4. Yosemite	_____	_____
5. appetite	_____	_____
6. bring	_____	_____
7. too	_____	_____
8. tooth	_____	_____
9. advice	_____	_____
10. always	_____	_____

II. Write N above each common or proper noun. Use the noun test and your dictionary. (15 points, 3 points each)

1. Firefighters often must work long hours without a break.
2. Our children play basketball at Garrison Recreational Center.
3. Khalida records her ideas daily in a journal.
4. Drivers sometimes need coins for the meter.
5. My roommate bought that lamp at a sale.

III. Each of the following sentences contains an error in the possessive form of a noun. Underline the error. Then write the correct form on the line at the right. (5 points, 1 point each)

1. Everyone laughs at my sister-in-laws jokes. _____
2. The storys conclusion was an unexpected one. _____
3. Many doctors offices are closed this afternoon. _____
4. Karens husband races stock cars on the weekend. _____
5. The pilots strike has been settled. _____

IV. Change the underlined nouns to the possessive form. Write the possessive form on the line at the right. (10 points, 2 points each)

1. the home of Mrs. <u>Sanchez</u> _____
2. the journals that belong to the <u>students</u> _____
3. the computer of my <u>boss</u> _____
4. the hats that belong to the <u>men</u> _____
5. the name of my <u>brother-in-law</u> _____

V. Each of the following sentences contains a shift in a personal pronoun. Identify each error by drawing a line under the incorrect pronoun. Write the correct form on the line at the right. (10 points, 2 points each)

1. A mockingbird is very protective of its young. They will swoop down to attack anyone beneath the nest.   _____
2. If a friend offers you a ride home, you should be sure to thank them.   _____
3. Roller blading is my favorite sport. You enjoy a wonderful feeling of freedom. _____
4. Physicians should be on time and not keep your patients waiting.   _____
5. When a player hits a home run with the bases loaded, the fans applaud them wildly.   _____

VI. Correct the spelling errors in the underlined pronoun forms. (10 points, 2 points each)

1. Who's photographs won first prize?   _____
2. The bird flew out of it's cage.   _____
3. Your group's reports are scheduled after theirs'.   _____
4. You're name is hard for me to pronounce.   _____
5. You heard his story, but you haven't listened to our's.   _____

VII. Write two sentences using the possessive form of singular nouns. Write three sentences using the possessive form of plural nouns. (15 points, 3 points each)

1._____

_____

_____

2._____

_____

_____

3._____

_____

_____

4._____

_____

_____

5._____

_____

_____

VIII. Write the PLURAL forms of the following nouns. (10 points, 2 points each)

1. watch   _____
2. boss   _____
3. path   _____
4. cash   _____

5. duty _____

IX. If the use of the underlined pronoun is correct, write C on the line. If the use of the pronoun is incorrect, write the correct pronoun on the line. (5 points, 1 point each)

1. The model liked reading about <u>herself</u> in fashion magazines. _____
2. My wife and <u>myself</u> are planning a trip. _____
3. He told <u>hisself</u> he would win the playoff _____
4. We spent the day by <u>ourselfs.</u> _____
5. They tired <u>themselves</u> out by shopping all day. _____

Chapter 2 Test: Verbs
Form A

Name _____
Date _____ Class Time _____
Instructor _____

I. Underline the verb. Write the past tense form of each verb on the line at the right. (15 points, 3 points each)

1. They like vacations in the mountains.   _____
2. Christina usually rides her bike to school.   _____
3. Anthony buys accessories for his bike at K-Mart.   _____
4. Mountain biking is his favorite form of exercise.   _____
5. Anthony looks at biking magazines every month.   _____

II. Underline the main verbs twice and the auxiliary verbs once. Some sentences may have no auxiliary verb, and some sentences may have more than one auxiliary verb. (20 points, 2 points each)

1. Lori could not remember Danielle's new address.
2. What were they arguing about?
3. The manager listened patiently to Brad's explanation.
4. Have you ever visited the city's aerospace museum?
5. Schools and county offices are not open today.
6. Our band will give a concert in the park Sunday.
7. Vicki had never been to a football game until last night.
8. Ariela has made the right choice.
9. The governor vetoed the housing bill.
10. I must have lost my wallet in the market.

III. Write auxiliary verbs in the blanks to make complete sentences. (10 points, 2 points each)

1. My sister _____ already tried one fad diet after another.
2. Tien Ho _____ learning English quickly.
3. Mr.Lee _____ help the students with their assignments tomorrow.
4. _____ you going to class now?
5. Rita _____ already filled the orders.

IV. Complete the following sentences with the future tense of the verb in parentheses. (10 points, 2 points each)

1. (win) Orlando knows that he _____ _____ the race.
2. (drive) All next month I _____ _____ you to work.
3. (understand) The instructor said that we _____ _____ the new lesson.
4. (play) The team _____ _____ at home for the next two games.
5. (have) Mr. Gomez _____ _____ a new partner next year.

V. In the following sentences, supply an auxiliary verb and a main verb using the verb in parentheses. Use one of the perfect tenses. (10 points, 2 points each)

1. (break) The test pilot _____ _____ the sound barrier while he was flying over the mountains.
2. (fix) The repairman surely _____ _____ _____ the television set by next Saturday.
3. (eat) After the family _____ _____ a picnic lunch, they walked to the lake.
4. (go) The children _____ just _____ to the zoo.
5. (teach) Mr. Able _____ _____ an evening class for the past ten years.

VI. Write the principal forms of the following verbs. (20 points, 1 point each)

Present	Present + s	Past	Past Participle	Present Participle
1. choose	_____	_____	_____	_____
2. suppose	_____	_____	_____	_____
3. carry	_____	_____	_____	_____
4. drink	_____	_____	_____	_____
5. am, are	_____	_____	_____	_____

VII. In the following sentences, bracket the adverbs and the contractions. Then underline the main verbs twice and the auxiliary verbs once. (15 points, 3 points each)

1. Do you still live at this address?
2. The street has just been closed for repairs.
3. Rescue efforts were further complicated by the storm.
4. The clerk has almost finished the inventory.
5. Hasn't Jana already made a reservation for us?

Chapter 2 Test: Verbs
Form B

Name _____
Date _____ Class Time _____
Instructor _____

I. Underline the verb. Write the past tense form of each verb on the line at the right. (15 points, 3 points each)

1. On Wednesdays, Mrs. Landis teaches an accounting class.   _____
2. She always explains the instructions clearly.   _____
3. The runner slides into third base.   _____
4. Gloria often travels to Central America.   _____
5. Is May 3rd your birthday?   _____

II. Underline the main verbs twice and the auxiliary verbs once. Some sentences may have no auxiliary verb, and others may have more than one auxiliary verb. (20 points, 2 points each)

1. The performance is ending now.
2. Tony had bought front-row seats.
3. That singing group has recorded another hit song.
4. We saw Angela at the basketball game.
5. The fans have been standing patiently in line.
6. Did you see that jump shot?
7. Caroline is making all the baskets from the free-throw line.
8. The team had won twenty games this season.
9. May I borrow your skateboard?
10. Tim worries about his car payments.

III. Fill in auxiliary verbs in the blanks to make complete sentences. (10 points, 2 points each)

1. Enrico _____ sung frequently at school dances.
2. Alysha_____ learned recently to use a computer.
3. Who_____cooking dinner tonight?
4. Max _____ already started the barbecue.
5. That dog _____ just eaten our steak!

IV. Complete the following sentences with the future tense of the verb in parentheses. (10 points, 2 points each)

1. (compete) Cheryl _____ _____ in two events tomorrow.
2. (begin) Competition _____ _____ tomorrow.
3. (drive) Bob said that he _____ _____ us to the field trials.
4. (win) Some people say that he _____ _____ a gold medal.
5. (be) The coach predicted that Ignacio _____ _____ the fastest runner in the race.

V. In the following sentences, supply an auxiliary verb and a main verb using the verb in parentheses. Use one of the perfect tenses. (10 points, 2 points each)

1. (make) _____ Mr. Lombardo _____ his plane reservations for Dallas?
2. (arrive) By last Tuesday, everyone _____ _____ at the conference.
3. (attend) If Juan goes to the meeting in Toronto, he _____ _____ _____
four conferences in the last six weeks.
4. (forget) Yesterday Yukio arrived at work late because he _____ _____ to set
his alarm.
5. (be) He _____ _____ at the office until late every night this week.

VI. Write the principal forms of the following verbs. (20 points, 1 point each)

Present	**Present +s**	**Past**	**Past Participle**	**Present Participle**
1. am, are	_____	_____	_____	_____
2. write	_____	_____	_____	_____
3. put	_____	_____	_____	_____
4. lose	_____	_____	_____	_____
5. reply	_____	_____	_____	_____

VII. In the following sentences, bracket the adverbs and the contractions. Then underline the main verbs twice and the auxiliary verbs once. (15 points, 3 points each)

1. Ruben has just given his daughter a birthday present.
2. Sophie has never been so excited about a gift.
3. Hasn't she ever ridden a bicycle?
4. Sophie is actually riding into that hedge.
5. The little girl didn't even cry.

Chapter 2 Test: Verbs
Form C

Name _____
Date _____ Class Time _____
Instructor _____

I. Underline the verb. Write the past tense form of each verb on the line at the right. (15 points, 3 points each)

1. Maria washes all her clothes at the Laundromat.   _____
2. I send my wool clothes to the cleaners.   _____
3. That switch turns the light on.   _____
4. Andrea sells shoes at the department store.   _____
5. The nurse gives first aid lessons.   _____

II. Underline the main verbs twice and the auxiliary verbs once. Some sentences may have no auxiliary verbs, and others may have more than one auxiliary verb. (20 points, 2 points each)

1. You must be Dr. Mason.
2. Does our plan suit you?
3. The picture is not for sale.
4. Simone and Angelo are riding their bicycles from Oregon to Virginia.
5. Should we order dinner now?
6. The chef at the restaurant can prepare delicious soups.
7. Charles may have left the office early.
8. Should we take umbrellas to work today?
9. Paul has been a bus driver for three years.
10. Everyone is talking about the rising cost of living.

III. Write auxiliary verbs in the blanks to make complete sentences. (10 points, 2 points each)

1. Lupe _____ dancing to the flamenco music.
2. My uncle _____ known his business partner for over twenty-five years.
3. _____ you ever played the lottery?
4. They _____ shopping for a new compact disc player.
5. Anthony _____ travel to Atlanta with the basketball team tomorrow.

IV. Complete the following sentences with the future tense of the verb in parentheses. (10 points, 2 points each)

1. (forgive) Ana _____ never _____ Ron now.
2. (train) The company _____ _____ three new employees.
3. (wilt) Put the flowers in water, or they _____ _____.
4. (choose) The presidential candidate announced that he _____ _____ his running mate tomorrow.
5. (study) I decided that I _____ _____ later.

V. In the following sentences, supply an auxiliary verb and a main verb using the verb in parentheses. Use one of the perfect tenses. (10 points, 2 points each)

1. (audition) The director _____ _____ ten children for the part before she chose Tim.
2. (travel) Mr. Turner _____ _____ _____ four thousand miles by the time the plane lands in Hawaii.
3. (try) _____ you _____ to solve the problems in the algebra assignment?
4. (bring) Rosalba _____ _____ two bags on oranges to her friend in the hospital.
5. (see) Dale _____ already _____ that movie five times.

VI. Write the principal forms of the following verbs. (20 points, 1 point each)

Present	Present +s	Past	Past Participle	Present Participle
1. have	_____	_____	_____	_____
2. buy	_____	_____	_____	_____
3. hurry	_____	_____	_____	_____
4. am, are	_____	_____	_____	_____
5. bring	_____	_____	_____	_____

VII. In the following sentences, bracket the adverbs and the contractions. Then underline the main verbs twice and the auxiliary verbs once. (15 points, 3 points each)

1. My sister has often talked about her friend in Miami.
2. Wouldn't you rather stay home tonight?
3. After class Winston is usually waiting for us by the library.
4. Mr. Williams's tests can sometimes be difficult.
5. Mr. and Mrs. Tanase aren't returning home until later this month.

Chapter 3 Test: Understanding the Parts of the Sentence
Form A

Name _____
Date _____ Class Time _____
Instructor _____

I. Write the subjects, the auxiliary verbs, and the main verbs on the lines at the right. Some sentences may have more than one auxiliary verb, and some may not have any auxiliary verb. All the sentences have main verbs and subjects. (30 points, 1 point each answer)

	Subject	**Auxiliary Verb**	**Main Verb**
1. Check your paper for errors.	_____	_____	_____
2. The building has several empty offices.	_____	_____	_____
3. Who will win the World Series this year?	_____	_____	_____
4. Many of the stores are selling lottery tickets.	_____	_____	_____
5. Brenda's new car doesn't have a CD player.	_____	_____	_____
6. Did the packages finally arrive?	_____	_____	_____
7. My aunt has visited many countries.	_____	_____	_____
8. She once traveled around the world.	_____	_____	_____
9. The fire must have started about 2 A.M.	_____	_____	_____
10. After the earthquake, Joanne moved back to Newark.	_____	_____	_____

II. First, bracket the prepositional phrases and underline the verbs. Then write the word that is the object of the verb on the line at the right. If there is no object of the verb, leave the space blank. (15 points, 3 points each)

Object of verb

1. The drummer played a solo in the last set. _____
2. Has the shipment from Florida arrived yet? _____
3. Form a line alongside the theater to buy tickets. _____
4. The flight crew prepared for takeoff. _____
5. Sean wrote an essay about a frightening experience. _____

III. Write a word of your choice in each blank. The words that are called for are linking verbs (LV) and completers (C). Do not use any form of a verb more than once, including the verb to be (am, is, are, was, were). (10 points, 2 points each)

(LV) 1. Many drivers _____ impatient on the crowded highway.
(C) 2. Philip seemed _____ to be working as a real estate agent.
(LV) 3. Glenn _____ surprised by his promotion yesterday.
(C) 4. Miami is _____.
(C) 5. Why does Mr. Gabriel look so _____ ?

IV. 1. Write a sentence with a compound verb. (5 points)

_____

2. Write a sentence with a compound subject. (5 points)

_____

_____

3. Write a sentence with a compound object or a compound completer. (5 points)

_____

_____

V. In the following sentences, underline the correct form of the pronoun in parentheses. (10 points, 2 points each)

1. My sister and (I, me) have been playing golf on Saturdays.
2. After our golf game, I'm going shopping with Marcel and (she, her).
3. No one in Bart's marketing class had any sales experience except Julie and (he, him).
4. No one wanted to go to the hockey match except Taylor, Carin, Nick and (I, me).
5. This fall Kelly and Abby applied to several colleges for admission. Both Kelly and (she, her) used the Internet to apply.

VI. In the following sentences, bracket the prepositional phrases. (5 points, 1 point each)

1. A stalled car in the middle of the bridge slowed traffic for a long time.
2. All of us waited impatiently because of the traffic jam.
3. The cars moved cautiously through the dark despite the icy wind and rain.
4. After the storm, the traffic on the bridge improved.
5. On account of the delay, many of the drivers arrived home late.

VII. a. Supply the missing apostrophe. (5 points, 1 point each)

1. Hes leaving for New York City tonight.
2. Theyre also going on vacation soon.
3. Shell drive all of us to the airport.
4. Its about five miles away.
5. Theres the suitcase by the front door.

VII. b. Now write the subjects and the complete verbs of the sentences in VII. a. Omit the apostrophes and supply the missing letters of the verb if necessary. (10 points, 2 points each sentence)

Subject	Auxiliary Verb	Main Verb
1. _____	_____	_____
2. _____	_____	_____
3. _____	_____	_____
4. _____	_____	_____
5. _____	_____	_____

Chapter 3 Test: Understanding the Parts of the Sentence
Form B

Name _____

Date _____ Class Time _____

Instructor _____

I. Write the subjects, the auxiliary verbs, and the main verbs on the lines at the right. Some sentences may have more than one auxiliary verb, and some may not have any auxiliary verb, but all the sentences have main verbs and subjects. (30 points, 1 point each answer)

	Subject	Aux. Verb	Main Verb
1. I can hear band music.	_____	_____	_____
2. Come to the parade with us.	_____	_____	_____
3. Mr. Danner is leading our band.	_____	_____	_____
4. Renata has never marched with the band until today.	_____	_____	_____
5. We have been decorating our club's float since Friday.	_____	_____	_____
6. The drum major has just dropped his baton.	_____	_____	_____
7. One of the clowns has picked it up.	_____	_____	_____
8. Now the clown will twirl it.	_____	_____	_____
9. The crowd laughs and applauds.	_____	_____	_____
10. Don't you love a parade?	_____	_____	_____

II. First, bracket the prepositional phrases and underline the verbs. Then write the word that is the object of the verb on the line at the right. If there is no object of the verb, leave the space blank. (15 points, 3 points each)

	Object of verb
1. The speaker has been talking for an hour.	_____
2. Mark looks around the auditorium at his friends.	_____
3. Diane is reading a book of poetry.	_____
4. Is Ray actually taking notes during this lecture?	_____
5. When will she finish her speech?	_____

III. Write a word of your choice in each blank. The words that are called for are linking verbs (LV) and completers (C). Do not use any form of a verb more than once, including the verb "to be" (am, is, are, was, were). (10 points, 2 points each)

1. (C) Is Mrs. O'Hara your _____?
2. (LV) Wanda _____ pretty in her new black sweater.
3. (C) The story Everett told us sounds _____.
4. (LV) Dana thought that the chili _____ too spicy.
5. (C) Marcus became a _____ before he moved to Portland.

IV. 1. Write a sentence with a compound verb. (5 points)

_____

2. Write a sentence with a compound subject. (5 points)

_____

_____

3. Write a sentence with a compound object or a compound completer. (5 points)

_____

_____

V. In the following sentences, write the correct form of the pronoun on the line at the right. (10 points, 2 points each)

1. My neighbor and (I, me) served on the same jury last week.
2. Mr. Luciano will testify at the trial because no one except (he, him) saw the accident.
3. I first met Elizabeth when (her, she) and Fran sublet my apartment.
4. Four of us will speak at the meeting: Luis, Preston, Rochelle, and (me, I).
5. When Manny's car wouldn't start, we gave Steve and (he, him) a ride to school.

VI. In the following sentences, bracket the prepositional phrases. (5 points, 1 point each)

1. The students at the bookstore were complaining about the slow service.
2. The city has just installed a traffic light at the end of our block.
3. In spite of his injured arm, Matt played in the game today.
4. Barry is going to the gym with Dwight.
5. Some of the questions were too difficult for me.

VII. a. Supply the missing apostrophe. (5 points, 1 point each)

1. Its time for class.
2. Shes speaking to him right now.
3. Theyll answer my letter soon.
4. Were leaving at noon tomorrow.
5. Youre the best pole vaulter in the country.

VII. b. Now write the subjects and the complete verbs of the sentences in VII. a. Omit the apostrophes and supply the missing letters of the verb if necessary. (10 points, 2 points each sentence)

Subject	Auxiliary Verbs	Main Verb
1. _____	_____	_____
2. _____	_____	_____
3. _____	_____	_____
4. _____	_____	_____
5. _____	_____	_____

Chapter 3 Test: Understanding the Parts of the Sentence
Form C

Name _____
Date _____ Class Time _____
Instructor _____

I. Write the subjects, the auxiliary verbs, and the main verbs on the lines at the right. Some sentences may have more than one auxiliary verb, and some may not have any auxiliary verb, but all the sentences have main verbs and subjects. (30 points, 1 point each answer)

	Subject	Aux. Verb	Main Verb
1. Mr. Arana doesn't like crowds.	_____	_____	_____
2. Send the invitations soon!	_____	_____	_____
3. Is Pam enjoying her vacation?	_____	_____	_____
4. I can never read his writing.	_____	_____	_____
5. Would you lend me your book?	_____	_____	_____
6. Ava and Vic work as tour guides.	_____	_____	_____
7. Gino's cafe has just opened.	_____	_____	_____
8. That piano should be tuned.	_____	_____	_____
9. Our class has only ten students.	_____	_____	_____
10. The bookstore will have the workbook by Monday.	_____	_____	_____

II. First bracket the prepositional phrases. Then write the word that is the object of the verb on the line at the right. If there is no object of the verb, leave the space blank. (15 points, 3 points each)

	Object
1. Akira marked the date on the calendar.	_____
2. Don't forget it.	_____
3. Russ and I will visit Akira next month.	_____
4. Russ, my best friend, is staying with me.	_____
5. We will drive from Texas to Illinois on our trip.	_____

III. Write a word of your choice in each blank. The words that are called for are linking verbs (LV) and completers (C). Do not use any form of a verb more than once, including the verb "to be" (am, is, are, was, were). (10 points, 2 points each)

1. (C) Mr. Hurwitz is our_____ .
2. (LV) They_____cold and damp.
3. (C) Are those pears_____?
4. (LV) Your dog_____a pest.
5. (LV) Arnold_____tall and thin.

IV. 1. Write a sentence with a compound verb. (5 points)

_____

2. Write a sentence with a compound subject. (5 points)

_____

_____

3. Write a sentence with a compound object or a compound completer. (5 points)

_____

_____

V. In the following sentences, underline the correct form of the pronoun on the line at the right. (10 points, 2 points each)

1. Mary said that Beth and (her, she) have been accepted to the police academy.
2. Beth and Mary and (me, I) had applied to the academy in October.
3. Mary is very happy about the news. No one else received notice except Beth and (her, she).
4. Now I hope that the academy accepts Richard and (me, I).
5. The police academy officer told Richard that they would notify (him, he) and (me, I) soon.

VI. In the following sentences, bracket the prepositional phrases. (5 points, 1 point each sentence)

1. La Neisha Williams has been serving in the Navy aboard the U.S.S. Cole.
2. She has been at sea for three months.
3. Her tour of duty has taken her to the Middle East.
4. The U.S.S. Cole has traveled from Turkey to the port in Yemen.
5. Throughout the voyage, La Neisha has been corresponding with her family.

VII. a. Supply the missing apostrophe. (5 points, 1 point each)

1. Ive invited Marla and Jack to dinner Friday evening.
2. Theyll arrive about 6:30.
3. Wasnt Jack in your history class last semester?
4. Youre going to enjoy meeting Marla.
5. Jacks planning to bring two new videos to watch after dinner.

VII. b. Now write the subjects and the complete verbs of the sentences in VII. a. Omit the apostrophes and supply the missing letters of the verb if necessary. (10 points, 2 points each sentence)

Subject	Auxiliary Verbs	Main Verb
1. _____	_____	_____
2. _____	_____	_____
3. _____	_____	_____
4. _____	_____	_____
5. _____	_____	_____

Chapter 4 Test: Adjectives and Adverbs
Form A

Name _____

Date _____ Class Time _____

Instructor _____

I. Bracket all adjectives including noun markers in the following sentences. (30 points, 6 points each sentence)

1. Some test questions are easier than others.
2. We enjoyed warm, sunny weather during our vacation.
3. Mrs. Yasuda's accounting office is in this building.
4. Is the gas tank full?
5. That potato salad tastes too salty.

II. In the following sentences, bracket all the adverbs. Each sentence has one adverb. (10 points, 2 points each sentence)

1. Madelyn speaks Russian fluently.
2. Jack's dog seldom barks.
3. Did you ever get my message?
4. That jacket is too large.
5. The gift you sent yesterday was a surprise.

III. Change the adjective in parentheses into the comparative or superlative degree. (15 points, 3 points each sentence)

1. Mr. Glover is the _____ person on the staff. (understanding, superlative)
2. An orange has _____ calories than a candy bar. (few, comparative)
3. Megan is the _____ child in her class. (curious, superlative)
4. That magician has the _____ act we have ever seen. (amazing, superlative)
5. My headache is _____ now than it was an hour ago. (good, comparative)

IV. Change the adverb in parentheses into the comparative or superlative degree. (15 points, 3 points each)

1. Robert made his point _____. (emphatically, superlative)
2. Jonelle had to drive _____ to work when she changed jobs. (far, comparative)
3. Visitors can view the city _____ of all from Ridge Drive. (well, superlative)
4. As the visitors looked at the view, they walked _____than usual so they could take pictures of the city. (slowly, comparative)
5. After Mrs. Turner had broken a plate, she packed the dishes _____ than before. (carefully, comparative)

V. Underline the misplaced modifier in each sentence. Then rewrite the sentence, placing the modifier where it belongs. (15 points, 5 points each sentence)

1. We watched the tornado destroy everything in its path on the evening news.

_____

2. Mrs. Scott tried to remove the spot with a strong detergent in the carpeting.

_____

3. Mia watched the band marching in the parade through her office window.

_____

VI. Underline the dangling modifier in each sentence. Then revise the sentence by moving modifiers, adding words, or rewriting the sentence. (15 points, 5 points each sentence)

1. After working overtime for several months, a vacation was welcome to me.

_____

2. While repairing his fence, the hammer smashed Leon's finger.

_____

3. Impressed by the salesman's words, the motorcycle seemed an unusually good buy to Harley.

_____

Chapter 4 Test: Adjectives and Adverbs
Form B

Name _____
Date _____ Class Time _____
Instructor _____

I. Bracket all adjectives including noun markers in the following sentences. (30 points, 6 points each sentence)

1. My husband is wearing torn jeans and cowboy boots.
2. That woman's car has very bright headlights.
3. Every time Anthony comes home, he plays his new stereo.
4. We stopped to watch two street musicians and a juggler perform.
5. Those three young people entertained us.

II. In the following sentences, bracket the adverbs. Each sentence has one adverb. (10 points, 2 points each sentence)

1. Regina crossed the street carefully.
2. Yesterday the baseball team made four runs.
3. Lola has never tried to bake a wedding cake.
4. Casey sometimes sends his friends humorous greeting cards.
5. The students solved the math problem quickly.

III. Change the adjective in parentheses into the comparative or superlative degree. (15 points, 3 points each sentence)

1. Psychology is _____ than algebra for me to learn. (easy, comparative)
2. India is suffering through the _____ drought in its history. (bad, superlative)
3. Ricardo is the _____ sales representative in the company.
(successful, superlative)
4. Chocolate ice cream tastes _____ than vanilla ice cream. (good, comparative)
5. Rose comes from the _____ neighborhood in the city. (poor, superlative)

IV. Change the adverb in parentheses into the comparative or superlative degree. (15 points, 3 points each sentence)

1. Amalia learned to play tennis _____ after practicing with the coach.
(well, comparative)
2. The ruins in Peru have deteriorated _____ than those in Italy.
(badly, comparative)
3. Darrell completed the job _____ than the other workers.
(quickly, comparative)
4. The bicyclist who won the race rode the _____ of all. (fast, superlative)
5. The dentist says that I should brush my teeth _____ than I do.
(often, comparative)

modifier in each sentence. Then rewrite the sentence, placing the
points, 5 points each sentence)

d to leave his car by the side of the road.

_____

n the window of the mountain.

_____

3. Ruth nearly ate a pound of grapes by herself.

_____

VI. Underline the dangling modifier in each sentence. Then revise the sentence by moving the
modifiers, adding words, or rewriting the sentence. (15 points, 5 points each sentence)

1. Sitting too long in the sun, your skin can get sunburned.

_____

2. At the age of ten, my family traveled to Canada.

_____

3. Driving on Main Street, the traffic seemed heavy to Arnold.

_____

Chapter 4 Test: Adjectives and Adverbs
Form C

Name _____
Date _____ Class Time _____
Instructor _____

I. Bracket all adjectives including noun markers in the following sentences. (30 points, 6 points each sentence)

1. Is his bicycle green or blue?
2. Some office buildings have express elevators.
3. Their house has a tile roof.
4. This cord is worn and frayed.
5. Deanna's sister bought an expensive ring.

II. In the following sentences, bracket the adverbs. Each sentence has one adverb. (10 points, 2 points each sentence)

1. Andy often plays poker.
2. Caryn never buys cigarettes.
3. I studied math today.
4. Do you usually eat breakfast?
5. The rain was falling hard.

III. Change the adjective in parentheses into the comparative or superlative degree. (15 points, 3 points each sentence)

1. The sauce has the _____ flavor of all. (unusual, superlative)
2. These seats are _____ ones than we had at the last concert. (good, comparative)
3. The leader of the expedition is familiar with some of the _____ regions of central Asia. (isolated, superlative)
4. Lola realized that she must buy _____ shoes than the ones she was wearing. (comfortable, comparative)
5. She bought shoes made of the _____ leather she could find. (soft, superlative)

IV. Change the adverb in parentheses into the comparative or superlative degree. (15 points, 3 points each)

1. The Bensons received their tax refund _____ than they had expected. (soon, comparative)
2. Mrs. Williams can explain a math problem _____ than any other teacher can. (clearly, comparative)
3. As the crowd watched, the huge balloon rose _____ than the trees. (high, comparative)
4. Many people work _____ after lunch because the food makes them sleepy. (efficiently, comparative)
5. Dionne talks the _____ of anyone I have ever known. (fast, superlative)

70

V. Underline the misplaced modifier in each sentence. Then rewrite the sentence, placing the modifier where it belongs. (15 points, 5 points each sentence)

1. Mei listened for the telephone to ring expectantly.

_____

2. Ari ordered a sundae to go with whipped cream and nuts.

_____

3. Roz walked by while we were washing the car with her collie.

_____

VI. Underline the dangling modifier in each sentence. Then revise the sentence by moving the modifiers, adding words, or rewriting the sentence. (15 points, 5 points each sentence)

1. Visiting the zoo nursery, the young attendants were feeding the baby gorillas.

_____

2. My father bought me my first baseball glove when only a small child.

_____

3. While listening to the radio, the weatherman said that it would rain tomorrow.

_____

Chapter 5 Test: Main Clauses
Form A

Name _____

Date _____ Class Time _____

Instructor _____

I. On the lines at the right, write MC for main clause or P for phrase. (20 points, 4 points each)

1. Toby wanted to turn down the volume on the stereo _____
2. Hearing the same record over and over _____
3. For example: guitars, synthesizers, and drums _____
4. No one else in the house agreed with him _____
5. Telling the truth sometimes takes courage _____

II. Identify each sentence as simple or compound. (20 points, 4 points each)

1. The party, planned at the last moment, was a success. _____
2. Everyone enjoyed the food, the music, and the entertainment. _____
3. Running after the bus, he caught up to it and jumped aboard. _____
4. Juan's luggage was sent to Hawaii by mistake; in addition, he lost his wallet. _____
5. Dara and Alexei have left college to open a book store, but they'll return in the fall. _____

III. The following sentences contain words that can be used as adverbs or adverbial connectives. Begin by labeling the subjects and verbs. Write (S) for simple sentence or (C) for compound sentence on the lines at the right. Then punctuate the sentences correctly. (15 points, 3 points each)

1. Greg must become more familiar with city streets otherwise he may lose his job delivering pizzas. _____
2. Shalonda indeed feels encouraged by two promising job offers. _____
3. The apartment advertised in Sunday's paper was rented in fact by Monday morning. _____
4. Mr. Madrid spent Saturday morning cleaning out the garage however he won't be able to finish the job until next weekend. _____
5. He planned to take a short nap after lunch instead Mr. Madrid slept all afternoon. _____

IV. Underline the part of each sentence that is not in a parallel form. Then rewrite this part by making it parallel to the other items. (15 points, 3 points each sentence)

1. The world's largest skateboard park, which opened recently in Canada, has three separate areas: Intro Park, Central Park, and a Park for the Expert.

_____

2. Before the new public skate parks were built, skateboarders often damaged public property by jumping from park benches or to have jumped over street curbs.

_____

3. Cypress High School allows students not only to bring their skate boards to school, but also for using them as transportation to and from school.

_____

4. This California high school plans to install sixty skateboard racks and on charging the students ten dollars per year for their use.

5. Skateboarding's most famous athlete has become a millionaire by competing, owning his own skate company, and he markets his own popular video games.

V. The following sentences contain errors. Identify the error by writing CS (comma splice) or RO (run-on sentence) on the lines at the right. Then correct the sentences using the method suggested in parentheses. (30 points, 6 points each sentence)

1. We drove until midnight before stopping at a motel the next morning we were back on the road by 6 A.M. (coordinating connective) _____

2. The price of the ticket includes lunch, it will be served promptly after the meeting. (semicolon) _____

3. Mr. Hobson has been offered $30,000 for his collection of ceremonial masks he plans to donate them to a museum. (coordinating connective) _____

4. During the past five years, few new homes have been built in our neighborhood, many buyers are remodeling older houses. (adverbial connective) _____

Wayne had to replace the hard drive on his new computer fortunately the warranty covered the cost. (period and capital letter) _____

Chapter 5 Test: Main Clauses
Form B

Name _____

Date _____ Class Time _____

Instructor _____

I. On the lines at the right, write MC for main clause or P for phrase. (20 points, 4 points each)

1. Visiting the natural history museum   _____
2. Where is the sand-painting exhibit?   _____
3. Greeted by the docent   _____
4. The children ask many questions   _____
5. In five minutes, the museum is closing   _____

II. Identify each sentence as simple or compound. (20 points, 4 points each)

1. In spring the days become warmer, and we study outside on the campus.   _____
2. The students applauded the speaker, for she opposed any increase in tuition.   _____
3. After a long career, our basketball coach plans to retire this year.   _____
4. Many instructors, objecting to the school board's hiring policies, joined the union.   _____
5. I missed my midterm in anthropology, so I am taking a makeup exam next Tuesday.   _____

III. The following sentences contain words that can be used as adverbs or adverbial connectives. Begin by labeling the subjects and the verbs. Then write (S) for simple sentence or (C) for compound sentence on the lines at the right. Punctuate the sentences correctly. (15 points, 3 points each sentence)

1. Most Americans want to preserve their environment nevertheless few are willing to make the necessary personal sacrifices.   _____
2. Lyle wrote a letter to the governor however he didn't actually expect an answer.   _____
3. He was surprised therefore to receive a letter from her regarding the environment   _____
4. The governor furthermore invited him to visit the state capital during spring break.   _____
5. The plane was an hour late consequently Lyle nearly missed his connecting flight.   _____

IV. Underline the part of each sentence that is not in a parallel form. Then rewrite this part by making it parallel to the other items. (15 points, 3 points each sentence)

1. The Italian immigrant Simon Rodia constructed Watts Towers on a dead-end street, near railroad tracks, on a lot that is triangular.

_____

2. Rodia not only built this 992-foot sculpture by himself at night but also working as a plasterer and tile setter during the day.

_____

3. The spires of this folk-art masterpiece in Los Angeles were erected without the aid of machines, scaffolding, bolts, and had no rivets.

_____

4. The artist had to reinforce his structure with discarded steel rods and pipes and even using bed frames and other castoffs.

_____

_____

5. Visitors especially admire the decorative broken glass, sea shells, and tiles that are ceramic on the towers.

_____

_____

V. The following sentences contain errors. Identify the error by writing CS (comma splice) or RO (run-on sentence) on the line at the right. Then correct the sentences using the method suggested in parentheses. (30 points, 6 points each sentence)

1. I crossed the street in the middle of the block a police officer gave me a ticket for jaywalking. (coordinating connective) _____

_____

2. Monica won't graduate until June, she started working at her new job in May. (adverbial connective) _____

_____

3. Joe drove up and down the streets for ten minutes finally, he found a parking place. (semicolon) _____

_____

4. The mail carrier rang the doorbell several times, no one answered. (coordinating connective) _____

_____

5. Shereda was out of town on a business trip on Election Day she voted by absentee ballot. (adverbial connective) _____

_____

_____

Chapter 5 Test: Main Clauses
Form C

Name _____

Date _____ Class Time _____

Instructor _____

I. On the lines at the right, write MC for main clause or P for phrase. (20 points, 4 points each)

1. Drinking a cup of coffee between classes _____
2. Sit down _____
3. In a short time, Thomas had completed the puzzle _____
4. The guests discussing politics after dinner _____
5. Are you ready _____

II. Identify each sentence as simple or compound. (20 points, 4 points each)

1. Les sometimes goes to football games, but he prefers basketball. _____
2. Darla finally got up and turned off the television set; she had to study for her physics test. _____
3. A skilled lecturer and popular teacher, Dr. Oren is a leading American anthropologist. _____
4. They met in May and married just two months later in July. _____
5. The chairman called the meeting to order and asked the secretary to read the minutes of the last meeting, before moving on to the first item on the agenda. _____

III. The following sentences contain words that can be used as adverbs or adverbial connectives. Begin by labeling the subjects and verbs. Then write (S) for simple sentence or (C) for compound sentence on the lines at the right. Punctuate the sentences correctly. (15 points, 3 points each sentence)

1. The budget for the school band has been cut therefore the musicians must buy their own uniforms. _____
2. The President however lacked congressional support for his programs. _____
3. Chocolate cake is delicious however it is fattening. _____
4. The instructor wondered moreover about the low scores on all the tests. _____
5. Jada wasn't enjoying the film nevertheless she stayed until the end. _____

IV. Underline the part of each sentence that is not in a parallel form. Then rewrite this part by making it parallel to the other items. (15 points, 3 points each)

1. The Akashi Kaikyo Bridge in Japan is the largest, tallest, and costs the most of any suspension bridge in the world.

_____

_____

2. In designing the Akashi Bridge, engineers knew that taking the extreme weather into account was as important as not to block shipping traffic.

_____

_____

3. One of the four artificial islands on the Chesapeake Bay Bridge-Tunnel in Virginia offers drivers a parking lot, restrooms, a shop that sells gifts, and a scenic view.

4. Before the New River Gorge Bridge was built, travelers crossed the West Virginia gorge by making a 40-mile detour or had to drive down narrow mountain roads.

5. Now, drivers not only reduce their driving time to a minute, but also enjoying a beautiful view of the gorge.

V. The following sentences contain errors. Identify the errors by writing CS (comma splice) or RO (run-on sentence) on the lines at the right. Then correct the sentences using the method suggested in parentheses. (30 points, 6 points each sentence)

1. The cafeteria at our school is always crowded at noon we will have to eat there today. (adverbial connective) _____

2. Many children never see a large animal they must go to a zoo to see anything bigger than a dog. (semicolon) _____

3. Most movies I have seen lately show too much violence, I have to close my eyes. (coordinating connective) _____

4. Swallows used to nest at Mission San Juan Capistrano they now favor college buildings, overpasses, and storage firms. (adverbial connective) _____

5. The clock stopped, the instructor knew when to dismiss the class. (coordinating connective) _____

Chapter 6 Test: Subordinate Clauses
Form A

Name _____
Date _____ Class Time _____
Instructor _____

I. Place parentheses around the subordinator. Then underline the subordinate clause. (30 points, 6 points each sentence)

1. Mrs. Turner has just learned that she must move soon.
2. Although Mrs. Turner likes New Jersey, she will have to move to Florida.
3. She is going to move because her employer has opened a new office in Miami.
4. The Turners will rent an apartment while they are living in Miami.
5. The Turners will not sell their house in New Jersey until they buy one in Florida.

II. a. Change the following main clauses into subordinate clauses by adding a subordinator to the beginning of the clause. Do not use the same subordinator twice. (5 points, 1 point each)

1. _____ Fran doesn't like to ride in elevators
2. _____ she walked up the stairs instead
3. _____ Roger will meet her at the office
4. _____ they have finished work on the proposal
5. _____ Fran and Roger are partners

II. b. Make a complete sentence by adding a main clause to each subordinate clause you made above. Your sentence should include both clauses. (10 points, 2 points each sentence)

1. _____

_____

2. _____

_____

3. _____

_____

4. _____

_____

5. _____

_____

III. Write three sentences that have one main clause and at least one subordinate clause. Place parentheses around the subordinator. Punctuate the sentence correctly. (15 points, 5 points each sentence)

1. _____

_____

2. _____

_____

3. _____

_____

IV. Identify the following comma splices and run-on sentences on the lines at the right. Then join the ideas in the main clauses into a complex sentence by changing one main clause to a subordinate clause. Use the subordinator in the parentheses. (10 points, 2 points each)

1. (when) Julia's children visit the park they love to ride on the miniature train. _____

_____

2. (where) During high school Terrell went to the YMCA, he learned to swim. _____

_____

3. (while) Robin enjoys the sights and sounds of a large city Seth enjoys a quiet day in the country. _____

_____

4. (after) Last night Jamal returned from the meeting he read the newspaper before dinner. _____

_____

5. (because) Garth is transferring to the Art Center, he wants to become a graphic artist. _____

_____

V. a. There are five incomplete sentences in the following paragraph. Indicate on the lines below whether a sentence is complete (S) or a sentence fragment (F). (15 points, 3 points each sentence fragment)

1. Ever since Jennifer was sixteen years old. 2. She has wanted to be a news broadcaster. 3. She has enrolled in college. 4. To prepare herself for this career. 5. So far she has completed several basic courses. 6. Speech 1, English 1, Journalism 1, and Beginning Broadcasting. 7. She especially enjoys taking part in discussions about current issues, and she has participated in a number of nationally televised talk shows. 8. While appearing on these shows. 9. She has met several famous people. 10. One of them is a well-known newscaster. 11. Who has given her an important break. 12. He has secured an internship for her with a major television network; Jennifer is on her way.

1. _____ 2. _____ 3. _____ 4. _____ 5. _____ 6. _____
7. _____ 8. _____ 9. _____ 10. _____ 11. _____ 12. _____

V. b. On the lines below, rewrite the incomplete sentences that you have just identified as sentence fragments. Rewrite each one by combining it with another sentence next to it. (15 points, 3 points each sentence)

1. _____

2. _____

3. _____

4. _____

5. _____

Chapter 6 Test: Subordinate Clauses
Form B

Name _____

Date _____ Class Time _____

Instructor _____

I. Place parentheses around the subordinator. Then underline the subordinate clause. (30 points, 6 points each sentence)

1. The house that Becky has rented is near the campus.
2. Since she lives so close to the campus, she walks to her classes.
3. Next month when Leola moves in, she will share expenses with Becky.
4. Jordan wanted to know how he could improve his grades in algebra.
5. His counselor recommended two students who are tutors in the mathematics department.

II. a. Change the following main clauses into subordinate clauses by adding a subordinator to the beginning of the clause. Do not use the same subordinator twice. (5 points, 1 point each)

1. _____ the doorbell rang
2. _____ Yvonne had invited ten guests
3. _____ Jeff likes to cook for a large group
4. _____ Dinner will be ready in an hour
5. _____ We listened to Jeff's new CD's

II. b. Make a complete sentence by adding a main clause to each subordinate clause you have made above. Your sentence should include both clauses. (10 points, 2 points each sentence)

1. _____

   _____

2. _____

   _____

3. _____

   _____

4. _____

   _____

5. _____

   _____

III. Write three sentences that have one main clause and at least one subordinate clause. Place parentheses around the subordinator. Punctuate the sentence correctly. (15 points, 5 points each sentence)

1. _____

   _____

2. _____

3. _____

IV. Identify the following comma splices and run-on sentences on the lines at the right. Then join the ideas in the main clauses into a complex sentence by changing one main clause to a subordinate clause. Use the subordinator in the parentheses. (10 points, 2 points each sentence)

1. (while) The two younger children played a video game, their mother was fixing lunch.

_____   _____

_____

2. (who, omit she) Their oldest sister was reading she had a book review assigned for Monday.

_____   _____

_____

3. (after) Corey and Lamar had finished working, they wanted to see a movie.   _____

_____

4. (before) We returned home we checked out a video from the library.   _____

_____

5. (although) We both had seen the film before, we watched it to the end.   _____

_____

_____

V. a. There are five incomplete sentences in the following paragraph. Indicate on the lines below whether a sentence is complete (S) or a sentence fragment (F). (15 points, 3 points each sentence fragment)

1. In my job at a bank, I watch the people. 2. As they wait in line. 3. I enjoy meeting new and different people. 4. Although they rarely answer me. 5. I always greet them with a cheerful "Good morning." 6. I watch them scowl. 7. As they fill out the deposit slips. 8. Sometimes they mutter to themselves. 9. While they try to add the numbers. 10. Sometimes they complain about the slow service. 11. They all look relieved and happy. 12. When they leave the bank.

1. ____   2. ____   3. ____   4. ____   5. ____   6. ____
7. ____   8. ____   9. ____   10. ____   11. ____   12. ____

V. b. On the lines below, rewrite the incomplete sentences that you have just identified as sentence fragments. Rewrite each one by combining it with another sentence next to it. (15 points, 3 points each sentence)

1.
_____
_____

2.
_____
_____

3.
_____
_____

4.
_____
_____

5.
_____
_____

Chapter 6 Test: Subordinate Clauses
Form C

Name _____

Date _____ Class Time _____

Instructor _____

I. Place parentheses around the subordinator. Then underline the subordinate clause. (30 points, 6 points each sentence)

1. Ed listens to the radio while he is trying to study.
2. The book that you found belongs to Josephina.
3. After the farmer had bought the truck, he showed it to his neighbors.
4. Lisa was the only cheerleader who had dance training.
5. The program cannot begin until everyone has been seated.

II. a. Change the following main clauses into subordinate clauses by adding a subordinator to the beginning of the clause. Do not use the same subordinator twice. (5 points, 1 point each)

1. _____ the concert began
2. _____ her father bought her a computer
3. _____ Marvin won a football scholarship
4. _____ you empty the wastebasket
5. _____ my son developed a toothache

II. b. Make a complete sentence by adding a main clause to each subordinate clause you have made above. Your sentence should contain both clauses. (10 points, 2 points each sentence)

1. _____

_____

2. _____

_____

3. _____

_____

4. _____

_____

5. _____

_____

III. Write three sentences that have one main clause and at least one subordinate clause. Place parentheses around the subordinator. Punctuate the sentence correctly. (15 points, 5 points each sentence.)

1.

_____

_____

2.

_____

_____

3.

_____

_____

IV. Identify the following comma splices (CS) and run-on sentences (RO) on the lines at the right. Then join the ideas in the main clauses into a complex sentence by changing one main clause to a subordinate clause. Use the subordinator in the parentheses. (10 points, 2 points each sentence)

1. (even though) Kevin hasn't saved enough money for tuition he has been working all summer. _____

_____

2. (when) Laura is on vacation, she likes to read and to sleep late every morning. _____

_____

3. (since) Mike entered college in the fall he has less time for social activities. _____

_____

4. (that) The film won four awards, it is playing in a theater at the Cinema Center. _____

_____

5. (as) The football players ran out on the field, the band began to play. _____

_____

V. a. There are five incomplete sentences in the following paragraph. Indicate on the lines below whether a sentence is complete (S) or a sentence fragment (F). (15 points, 3 points each sentence fragment)

1. As a result of the recent floods, the small town of Chicumbane (Chee-cum-ban-ay) in Mozambique was destroyed. 2. Now that the Limpopo River has receded considerably. 3. Plans are to rebuild on higher ground. 4. The elevated highway was overtaken by the raging river. 5. Requiring two boat journeys and about a fifty-minute walk between breaks. 6. The area is a wide, flat expanse. 7. Exposed to the ocean wind. 8. The Indian Ocean is thirty miles east, so the journey is windy and the water choppy. 9. The powerful action of the river removed huge sections of asphalt pavement. 10. Lifted whole like ribbons of taffy and gently relocated downstream. 11. Still potent was the smell of a few cattle carcasses. 12. Which had been left to rot along the banks of the river.

1. ____ 2. ____ 3. ____ 4. ____ 5. ____ 6. ____

7. ____ 8. ____ 9. ____ 10. ____ 11. ____ 12. ____

V. b. On the lines below, rewrite the incomplete sentences that you have just identified as sentence fragments. Rewrite each one by combining it with another sentence next to it. (15 points, 3 points each sentence)

1._____

_____

2._____

_____

3._____

_____

4._____

_____

5._____

_____

_____

Chapter 7 Test: Agreement
Form A

Name _____

Date _____ Class Time _____

Instructor _____

I. Underline the correct verb. (20 points, 4 points each)

1. Cathy, along with other students, (has, have) been concerned about the heavy traffic near the school.
2. All the old cars on the streets (increase, increases) the smog.
3. There (is, are) at least ten things a driver can do to improve the quality of the air.
4. Keeping a car in good operating condition (contribute, contributes) to the reduction of particles in the atmosphere.
5. The home owner and the apartment renter now (use, uses) more efficient heating methods than in the past.

II. Underline the correct verb. (20 points, 4 points each)

1. Many people (apply, applies) for the scholarship.
2. None of the five applicants (is, are) qualified.
3. Seventy-five dollars (was, were) a high price for the application fee.
4. The winners of the scholarship (has, have) to maintain a B average.
5. Everyone in our class (work, works) hard to succeed.

III. Underline the correct pronoun. (20 points, 4 points each)

1. Either Jelena or Sondra will share (their, her) class notes with me.
2. The Pearson Book Company will discount (their, its) paperbacks on the Internet this month.
3. Neither Aramis nor Ben said that (he, they) would try out for the team.
4. The girls' drill team will have (its, their) fund-raising dance in February.
5. Byron, like several of his classmates, will spend (their, his) junior year studying abroad.

IV. Rewrite these sentences by giving unclear pronouns specific antecedents or by replacing the underlined pronouns with nouns. (20 points, 4 points each)

1. In large cities <u>they</u> have many violent crimes.

_____

_____

2. When the police officer stopped the traffic, <u>it</u> enabled the ambulance to get to the accident.

_____

_____

3. After Dennis talked to a helicopter pilot, he knew <u>this</u> was what he wanted as a job.

_____

_____

4. The final minutes of the game were very exciting, <u>which</u> made the crowd roar.

_____

_____

5. Lynnette told Kim that <u>her</u> paintings were beautiful.

_____

_____

V. Write your own sentences according to the instructions. (20 points, 5 points each)

1. Write a sentence beginning with the words, <u>There are</u>.

_____

2. Write a sentence using the word <u>physics</u> as the subject. Use a verb in the present tense.

_____

3. Write a sentence using <u>everyone</u> as the subject. Use a verb in the present tense.

_____

4. Write a sentence using <u>neither Mike nor the other men</u> as the subject of your sentence. Use a verb in the present tense.

_____

_____

Chapter 7 Test: Agreement
Form B

Name _____

Date _____ Class Time _____

Instructor _____

I. Underline the correct verb. (20 points, 4 points each)

1. After looking for several months, Rosa and Danny (has, have) rented an apartment in the older section of the city.
2. The apartment building, like others in that district, (appears, appear) to be in good condition despite its age.
3. The high ceilings of the newly painted, two-bedroom apartment (makes, make) it seem larger than it is.
4. There (is, are) shops, stores, and a bus stop within easy walking distance.
5. Three blocks down the street in the opposite direction (is, are) a small park with tennis courts and a play area for children.

II. Underline the correct verb. (20 points, 4 points each)

1. Mumps (is, are) a serious disease in adolescents.
2. (Has, have) either of these books been published in a soft cover edition?
3. Both of these self-help books (was, were) on the best-seller lists recently.
4. Everybody (likes, like) a bargain.
5. Where (is, are) the scissors?

III. Underline the correct pronoun in the following sentences. (20 points, 4 points each)

1. Both Scott and Marcus bring (his, their) children to the day-care center.
2. Mrs. Makeba, as well as several friends, did (their, her) holiday shopping on the Internet this year.
3. The jury returned (its, their) verdict quickly.
4. Mr. Iyemura's company gives (its, their) employees one-month vacations.
5. Either Rachel or Lynn will lend us (her, their) coffee maker for the reception.

IV. Rewrite these sentences by giving the underlined pronouns specific antecedents, or by replacing the underlined pronouns with nouns. (20 points, 4 points each)

1. Wally and Burt discussed <u>his</u> plans for the future.

_____

2. Hank charged into a defensive player <u>which</u> was called a foul by the referee.

_____

3. Annette has seen the same movie ten times this month. <u>This</u> is a new world's record.

_____

4. When one lane of the freeway was closed for repairs, <u>it</u> was slow-moving.

_____

5. When <u>they</u> raised the rents, the tenants complained.

_____

V. Write your own sentences according to the instructions. (20 points, 5 points each)

1. Write a sentence beginning with the words, <u>There are</u>.

_____

2. Write a sentence using <u>neither Jasmin nor Derek</u> as the subject. Use a verb in the present tense.

_____

3. Write a sentence using the word <u>economics</u> as the subject. Use a verb in the present tense.

_____

4. Write a sentence using the word <u>nobody</u> as the subject. Use a verb in the present tense.

_____

Chapter 7 Test: Agreement
Form C

Name _____

Date _____ Class Time _____

Instructor _____

I. Underline the correct verb. (20 points, 4 points each)

1. Where (is, are) the instructions for this exercise?
2. There (was, were) buttons missing from his shirt.
3. In the hula, the motions of the dancer, as well as the chant, often (describe, describes) the beauty of Hawaii.
4. Taped to the door of the refrigerator (were, was) a grocery list, a diet plan, and a dozen family photos.
5. The fenders of Debbie's bicycle (looks, look) rusty.

II. Underline the correct verb. (20 points, 4 points each)

1. Neither of the contestants on the quiz show (have, has) given the right answer to the question.
2. Each of your papers (shows, show) improvement.
3. Once a month, the Library Commission (issues, issue) the results of its meetings.
4. Mathematics (is, are) the most difficult subject for me.
5. Lauren, like many teenagers, (argues, argue) with her parents.

III. Underline the correct pronoun in the following sentences. (20 points, 4 points each)

1. Both Kay and Consuela bought (her, their) earrings at the student art fair.
2. Each of the girls designed (her, their) clothes for the fashion show.
3. Either Fred or Ben left (his, their) books in the cafeteria.
4. Dominic's Pizza will deliver (its, their) pizza to your home.
5. Many trees, like the maple, lose (their, its) leaves in the fall.

IV. Rewrite these sentences by giving unclear pronouns specific antecedents or by replacing the underlined pronouns with nouns. (20 points, 4 points each)

1. Linda is an excellent tutor. This is a rewarding occupation.

_____

_____

2. Their dog chases cars down the street which makes drivers nervous.

_____

_____

3. Kevin told Alberto that Harrison would meet him at the soccer field.

_____

_____

4. I like to eat in Chinese restaurants. They can be delicious.

_____

_____

5. Alan wanted a new leather jacket <u>which</u> made him work overtime for a month.

_____

_____

V. Write your own sentences according to instructions. (20 points, 5 points each)

1. Write a sentence using the word <u>trousers</u> as the subject. Use a verb in the present tense.

_____

2. Write a sentence using the word <u>everybody</u> as the subject. Use a verb in the present tense.

_____

3. Write a sentence using <u>either Jan or Mark</u> as the subject of your sentence. Use a verb in the present tense.

_____

4. Write a sentence beginning with the words <u>Here is.</u>

_____

_____

Chapter 8 Test: Commas
Form A

Name _____

Date _____ Class Time _____

Instructor _____

I. Insert commas where they are necessary. Some sentences may not require commas. (80 points, 4 points each)

1. Although the farm workers complained about the conditions they still had to pick the crops.
2. Delores Ramirez who is the congresswoman from our district has a record of supporting farm legislation.
3. The lawyers met with the protesters but they could not arrive at a settlement.
4. Three well-trained young lawyers met with the workers.
5. The workers were persuaded to stay on the job because they could not afford to go on strike.
6. "Jonathan when do you want to go to the airport?" the lawyer asked his partner.
7. Calling from a pay phone in the crowded airport Jonathan could not hear a word his wife was saying.
8. The farm worker wore torn dirty faded blue jeans.
9. The union's treasurer mailed the check to the law firm of Cabot and Lodge 2400 Beacon Street Boston Massachusetts.
10. A conference call helped to settle some of the problems and the workers were satisfied that progress had been made.
11. Yolanda was pleased to see that the post office a bookstore a supermarket a Laundromat and a pharmacy were all within easy walking distance of her new apartment.
12. After she had moved in she enrolled in the local community college.
13. The fall semester began conveniently for her on September 14 2005 and ended on January 22 2006.
14. She was happy to learn moreover that she could place her young son in the college child-care center.
15. Yolanda also hoped to find a part-time job so she checked the opportunities in the placement center.
16. The Hillside Pharmacy which was located on the corner of Prospect Avenue was advertising for new employees.
17. To reach the pharmacy she had to walk only four blocks.
18. She learned two days after the interview that she could start her new job the next week.
19. Working would cut down on her study time but Yolanda was determined to succeed.
20. She celebrated by taking her son to his favorite restaurant for a big juicy hamburger and some crisp golden French fries.

II. Following the directions, write sentences of your own. (20 points, 5 points each)

1. Write a sentence containing two main clauses connected by a coordinating connective. Punctuate the sentence correctly.

_____

2. Write a sentence containing three or more adjectives that modify the same noun. Punctuate the sentence correctly.

_____

3. Write a sentence that contains an introductory phrase or an introductory subordinate clause. Punctuate the sentence correctly.

_____

4. Write a sentence that contains a complete address, including the city, the state, and the zip code. Punctuate the sentence correctly.

_____

_____

Chapter 8 Test: Commas
Form B

Name _____

Date _____ Class Time _____

Instructor _____

I. Insert commas where they are necessary. Some sentences may not require commas. (80 points, 4 points each)

1. The coach asked the players to bring their jerseys shorts knee pads and mouth guards to every practice session.
2. To get to the new gym turn left at the water fountain.
3. "Wait a minute Alex" the cheerleader called "and I'll go with you."
4. The team played its best game on March 13 but it was too late to qualify for the trophy.
5. Harris looked for an apartment on High Street because he wanted to live near the campus.
6. We were invited to the post-game celebration of course.
7. The players who were at the party enjoyed the refreshments.
8. The apple pie especially appealed to the hungry muscular basketball players.
9. Harris ate a sandwich and he was still able to eat two pieces of apple pie for dessert.
10. When Dana and Audrey arrived at the party they learned that the food was all gone.
11. Eliot Adams whose goal is to be a news photographer usually has his camera with him.
12. "I never know" he says "when a photo opportunity will come my way."
13. The regional basketball playoff indeed gave him that opportunity.
14. The center scored a slam dunk over two aggressive defenders during the final seconds of the game.
15. Eliot took the picture at just the right moment and his camera caught the game-winning play at the peak of action.
16. He sent his photograph to the Los Angeles Post 2565 State Street Los Angeles California 91074 as an entry in its annual photographic competition.
17. The photo placed first in the sports category but best of all it appeared in the Sunday paper.
18. To win this prize Eliot had competed against many talented photographers.
19. On the following Monday he located an art supply store at 1052 E. Merrill Avenue by looking in the yellow pages.
20. Eliot bought mat board a mat cutter aluminum framing a piece of precut glass and mounting board there to frame his prize-winning photograph.

II. Following the directions, write sentences of your own. (20 points, 5 points each)

1. Write a sentence containing two main clauses joined by a coordinating connective. Punctuate the sentence correctly.

_____

_____

2. Write a sentence containing three or more adjectives that modify the same noun. Punctuate the sentence correctly.

_____

_____

3. Write a sentence that contains an introductory phrase or an introductory subordinate clause. Punctuate the sentence correctly.

_____

4. Write a sentence that contains a complete address, including the city, the state, and the zip code. Punctuate the sentence correctly.

_____

_____

Chapter 8 Test: Commas
Form C

Name _____
Date _____ Class Time _____
Instructor _____

I. Insert commas where they are necessary. Some sentences may not require commas. (80 points, 4 points each)

1. Phil stopped working and took a nap.
2. Kwan put two books several pens a notebook and a calculator in the briefcase.
3. The coffee mug that I just bought is already cracked.
4. "Denise please lend me some compact discs" Marcus said "for the party tomorrow night."
5. The voter addressed her letter to the President the White House Washington D.C. 20500.
6. The bike path is crowded in the afternoon so we ride early in the morning.
7. Sol was excited when the employment agency called with a job offer.
8. Mi Lee does not come to work as a rule until noon.
9. On June 17 2004 our son graduated from college.
10. The class schedules for next semester are available in the Admissions Office but I don't have one yet.
11. Following instructions carefully Mario assembled the bicycle.
12. The tour leaves for Istanbul on August 2nd.
13. The runner suffered a pulled hamstring. He continued nevertheless to the finish line.
14. Thomas A. Edison who was a famous American inventor is often called the Wizard of Menlo Park.
15. After Susanna had swum twenty laps in the pool she felt refreshed.
16. In the trash can was Bradley's missing glove.
17. The enthusiastic loyal football fans sat in the cold rain until the end of the game.
18. For the past two months Ben has jogged three miles every day.
19. Mt. McKinley which is the highest mountain in North America is 20,320 feet high.
20. Nick Nolte plays a tough hard-driving rookie cop in the film.

II. Following the directions, write sentences of your own. (20 points, 5 points each)

1. Write a sentence containing two main clauses joined by a coordinating connective. Punctuate the sentence correctly.

_____

_____

2. Write a sentence containing three or more adjectives that modify the same noun. Punctuate the sentence correctly.

_____

_____

3. Write a sentence that contains an introductory phrase or an introductory subordinate clause. Punctuate the sentence correctly.

_____

_____

4. Write a sentence that contains a complete address, including the city, the state, and the zip code. Punctuate the sentence correctly.

_____

_____

Chapter 9 Test: Usage, Punctuation, and Sentence Mechanics
Form A

Name _____

Date _____ Class Time _____

Instructor _____

I. Add periods, question marks, or exclamation points to the following sentences. (15 points, 3 points each sentence)

1. Mr Jackson asked his wife how long she had been waiting
2. "He was safe by a mile" the coach yelled at the umpire
3. The plane leaves Los Angeles at 11:15 A M and arrives in Portland at 2:12 P M
4. Dr Tan received his D D S degree from U S C ten years ago.
5. "May I help you" the saleswoman asked

II. Insert semicolons and colons where they are needed in the following sentences. Do not remove commas. (15 points, 3 points each sentence)

1. My lab partner and I were puzzled the results of our chemistry experiment were certainly unexpected.
2. Melissa's calendar for the week included three important dates her sister's birthday, a dental appointment, and a friend's wedding.
3. Rhonda dialed the store's toll-free number she wanted to inquire about the sale of ten-speed bicycles.
4. While waiting to see the doctor, Jim had time to look through several magazines <u>Time</u>, <u>Ebony</u>, <u>People</u>, and <u>Sports Illustrated</u>.
5. Seat belts can reduce the chances of serious injury however, many drivers refuse to buckle up.

III. Capitalize where necessary. (15 points, 3 points each sentence)

1. last winter my father went to a conference in cancun, mexico.
2. the third sunday in june has been designated as father's day.
3. captain hardesty of the police department teaches a class at Larchmont community college.
4. can you name the presidents whose likenesses are carved on mt. rushmore?
5. bing cherries and thompson seedless grapes make perfect food for a picnic.

IV. Underline the errors in abbreviations and numbers. Then write the correct forms on the line following the sentence. (15 points, 3 points each sentence)

1. Planning a hiking trip with 3 friends to the Great Smoky Mts, Maria bought a new backpack for seventy-nine dollars and fifty cents.

_____

2. Dachelle's 1st class for the fall semester meets at 9 A M on Monday, Sept 10.

_____

3. 500 concert tickets had been sold by noon to the fans who had been waiting at the corner of Market Ave and State St for several hours.

_____

4. Sen Robert C. Byrd of W Virginia has served in the U.S. Senate since 1959.

_____

5. Ms Stewart's diet breakfast included a blueberry muffin (316 calories), an orange (sixty-two calories), and a glass of fat-free milk (eighty-six calories).

_____

V. For each word listed below, write a sentence of your own using that word correctly. (40 points, 4 points each sentence)

1. used

_____
_____

2. then

_____
_____

3. too

_____
_____

4. led

_____
_____

5. lose

_____
_____

6. it's

_____
_____

7. led

_____
_____

8. dessert

_____
_____

9. already

_____
_____

10. loose

_____
_____

Chapter 9 Test: Usage, Punctuation, and Sentence Mechanics
Form B

Name _____
Date _____ Class Time _____
Instructor _____

I. Add periods, question marks, or exclamation points to the following sentences. (15 points, 3 points each sentence)

1. The letter was addressed to Ms Cheryl Kam
2. Dr Barnes' office opens at 9 A M and closes at 5 P M
3. Al asked Janet if she liked her new job
4. Don't ever say that again
5. "Is the can opener in the picnic basket" he asked

II. Insert semicolons and colons where they are needed in the following sentences. Do not remove commas. (15 points, 3 points each sentence)

1. As a student worker in the library, Megan has a variety of duties shelving books, filing, technical processing, and working at the circulation desk.
2. Van will be forty next month however he has no idea that his friends are planning a surprise party for him.
3. When Shauna read the letter, she was pleasantly surprised the magazine had accepted her short story for publication.
4. Mr. Korach is a sales representative for an international company therefore, he travels to many different countries.
5. George took the following supplies to his drawing class four pencils of various grades, a pad of 24 x 36-inch paper, a kneaded eraser, and a chamois cloth.

III. Capitalize where necessary. (15 points, 3 points each sentence)

1. delores works on sundays, but she has wednesdays off.
2. granny smith apples are one of new zealand's exports.
3. i dropped my sociology class, but i am still enrolled in spanish and english.
4. valerie lives across the street from martin luther king high school.
5. in august we camped near lake louise.

IV. Underline the errors in abbreviations and numbers. Then write the correct forms on the line following the sentence. (15 points, 3 points each sentence)

1. At the end of the 3rd quarter, the score was twenty-one to twenty in favor of U.S.C.

_____

2. After working for Thompson Bros for 2 years, Latifa was pleased to learn that she would receive a seven-percent wage increase.

_____

3. Mrs. Sevedra read an article about N Korea in a recent issue of the Wall St Journal.

_____

4. When Prof Crane was 22, he dreamed of writing a best-selling novel in five or 10 years.

_____

5. Martin Luther King, Jr, civil rights leader, was born in Atlanta, Ga, on Jan 15, 1929.

V. For each word listed below, write a sentence of your own using that word correctly. (40 points, 4 points each sentence)

1. though

2. desert

3. principle

4. than

5. affect

6. know

7. past

8. supposed

9. its

10. through

Chapter 9 Test: Usage, Punctuation, and Sentence Mechanics
Form C

Name _____

Date _____ Class Time _____

Instructor _____

I. Add periods, question marks, or exclamation points to the following sentences. (15 points, 3 points each sentence)

1. Everyone always asks me how much I weigh
2. "Would you like tea or coffee" the waitress asked
3. Thomas received an A A degree last June
4. "Watch out for the truck" Louanne's mother cried
5. We are going to Washington, D C, next spring

II. Insert semicolons and colons where they are needed in the following sentences. Do not remove commas. (15 points, 3 points each sentence)

1. The grocery list contained the following items potatoes, lettuce, oranges, and milk.
2. Elena plans to run in the Boston Marathon therefore, she is training every day.
3. Martin has entered the track meet scheduled for tomorrow he hopes to win the 100-meter dash
4. Arianna wrote an article about the recent debates on TV in which she mentioned the following points the candidates' apparent lack of knowledge and their inability to express themselves clearly.
5. We have to buy a new car repairing our old one would be too expensive.

III. Capitalize where necessary. (15 points, 3 points each sentence)

1. annika said that the water in lake superior is cold even in the summer.
2. although she is an italian citizen, francesca has a home in southern california.
3. while visiting her grandmother in san francisco, jalena drove across the golden gate bridge.
4. terrell rented a ford explorer from mac's car rental.
5. on july 4th i I usually take the long island railroad to jones beach.

IV. Underline the errors in abbreviations and numbers. Then write the correct forms on the line following the sentence. (15 points, 3 points each sentence)

1. Capt Roberta Jackson has been stationed at Ft Lewis, Wash, since November.

_____

2. The author's work includes 110 short stories, two biographies, four travel books, and twelve novels.

_____

3. Although the plane landed on time at 10:50 PM, Mr Moritaki had to spend an hour locating his 3 suitcases.

_____

4. Gov Cappello introduced the main speaker of the session, Asst US Attorney Johnson.

_____

5. I paid three-hundred and eighty-seven dollars for a new storage unit at Mason Furniture Co and a delivery fee of twenty-five dollars.

_____

V. For each word listed below, write a sentence of your own using that word correctly. (40 points, 4 points each sentence.)

1. advise

_____

_____

2. except

_____

_____

3. who's

_____

_____

4. through

_____

_____

5. you're

_____

_____

6. all ready

_____

_____

7. effect

_____

_____

8. though

_____

_____

9. personal

_____

_____

Midterm Exam

(100 points, 5 points each)

Name _____

Date _____ Class Time _____

Instructor _____

I. Each of the following sentences contains an error in the <u>possessive form</u> of a noun or a pronoun. Underline each error. Write the correct form on the line at the right.

1. The gorillas cages are located at the south end of the zoo.   _____
2. The womens' car keys were in their purses.   _____
3. Are these books your's?   _____
4. When will Jennifers picture be printed in the paper?   _____
5. John shares his fathers' interest in science fiction.   _____

II. Fill in the blank with an appropriate form of the <u>verb</u> given in parentheses. It may be a main verb, or it may be a main verb and an auxiliary verb. Use the tense given in parentheses.

1. (finish) The painter has promised that he _____ _____ the work by Friday. (future tense)
2. (bring) Margaret _____ _____ her dictionary to class every day this week. (present perfect tense)
3. (forget) Justin was worried that he _____ _____ the time of the meeting. (future tense)
4. (swim) Last week Aaron _____ five laps in the pool. (past tense)
5. (give) Returning home, Marilyn realized that the salesman _____ _____ her someone else's package. (past perfect tense)

III. Write the <u>subject</u>, the <u>auxiliary verb</u>, and the <u>main verb</u> of each of the following sentences on the lines at the right. Some sentences may have more than one auxiliary verb; others may not have any auxiliary verb.

	Subject	Aux.Verb(s)	Main Verb
1. Which movie should we see tonight?	_____	_____	_____
2. William has been chosen for the debating team.	_____	_____	_____
3. Turn left at the next intersection.	_____	_____	_____
4. From her second-floor window, Ashley was able to see the sunset on the lake.	_____	_____	_____
5. All of us must make our reservations by next Friday.	_____	_____	_____

IV. a. Rewrite each of the following sentences to correct the **misplaced modifier**.

1.   Skating through the park, the breeze felt cool to Brenda on a warm day.

_____

_____

2. Sue works for her brother who is a lawyer after school.

_____

_____

IV. b. Rewrite each of the following sentences to correct the **dangling modifier**.

1. At the age of sixteen, a magazine published John's first short story.

_____

_____

2. After running around the track three times, a cool drink tasted delicious to Jamal.

_____

_____

3. Having served in World War I, *A Farewell To Arms* grew out of Hemingway's Italian army experiences.

_____

_____

Final Exam

(100 points)

Name _____

Date _____ Class Time _____

Instructor _____

I. a. Each of the following sentences contains an error in the <u>possessive form</u> of a noun or a pronoun. Underline each error. Write the correct form on the line at the right. (10 points, 2 points each)

1. I found someones watch in the library.   _____
2. Mr. Adams duties include counseling students.   _____
3. Todays professional athletes earn high salaries.   _____
4. Kirk was the clubs choice to be a delegate to the convention.   _____
5. Mens shirts are on sale at the store.   _____

I. b. Fill in the blank with an appropriate form of the <u>verb</u> given in parentheses. It may be a main verb, or it may be a main verb and an auxiliary verb. Use the tense given in parentheses. (10 points, 2 points each)

1. (stop) John hoped that the rain _____ _____ soon. (future tense)
2. (fall) Rose _____ just _____ asleep when the telephone rang. (past perfect tense)
3. (choose) Dennis _____ his courses carefully last semester. (past tense)
4. (repair) By next month, Mr. Johnson _____ _____ _____ the problem with the television. (future perfect tense)
5. (speak) The manager _____ already _____ to us about the problem. (present perfect tense)

II. a. Rewrite each of the following sentences to correct the **misplaced modifier**. (10 points, 2 points each)

1. The waitress in the Japanese restaurant brought rice to the diners in small covered containers.

_____

_____

2. Douglas shoots baskets with Kirby who is his neighbor nearly every Saturday afternoon.

_____

_____

II. b. Rewrite each of the following sentences to correct the **dangling modifier.**

1. Dropping the ball, the error was the second one of the game for Allen.

_____

_____

2. After leaving the bank, Calvin's ATM card was missing.

_____

_____

3. Determined to save money for my vacation, a budget seemed the best way to start.

_____

_____

III. Correct the following sentences, using the method suggested in parentheses. Use the correct punctuation. (20 points, 4 points each)

1. Luanne wanted to improve her serve, she enrolled in a tennis class this semester. (adverbial connective)

_____

_____

2. Some of the pictures were over-exposed, others were perfect. (semicolon)

_____

_____

3. I thought that a discussion group might be a waste of class time, the suggestions from the members of our group have helped me improve my writing. (coordinating connective)

_____

_____

4. My brother scrubbed and waxed the floor I washed the windows. (subordinate clause)

_____

_____

5. Cigarette smoking has been linked with lung cancer many people continue to smoke. (adverbial connective)

_____

_____

IV. Underline the correct word in parentheses. (10 points, 2 points each)

1. My husband and (I, myself) met for the first time in an accounting class.
2. Brian's glasses (needs, need) new lenses.
3. The Marco Company will begin the promotion of (their, its) new product next month.
4. The basketball team (are, is) playing in the gym tonight.
5. Two other builders, in addition to Mr. Campbell, (has, have) expressed an interest in buying the lots.

V. Insert <u>commas</u> where necessary in the following sentences. (10 points, 2 points each)

1. When the philharmonic performs Bradley sees every one of the concerts.
2. Forward my mail to 3356 Kern Avenue Canton Ohio.
3. Emily made the meatloaf with bread crumbs tomato sauce onions and ground beef.
4. On September 3 1998 John and Marie were married.
5. Toby Jackson who writes for the student paper plans to be a journalist.

VI. <u>Capitalize</u> and/or <u>punctuate</u> the following sentences correctly. (15 points, 3 points each)

1. while ben eats breakfast, he likes to read the newspaper
2. during the press conference, the secretary of state answered questions about relations with the following countries france, germany, japan, and poland
3. toby will interview senator mark russell at 2:30 P M today
4. i want to take a spanish class in the spring semester
5. taylor enjoyed the article about whitney houston in last month's issue of *ebony*

VII. Write a sentence of your own using each of the following words. (15 points, 3 points each)

1. Use the word <u>it's</u> in a sentence.

_____

_____

2. Use the word <u>effect</u> in a sentence.

_____

_____

3. Use the word <u>principle</u> in a sentence.

_____

_____

4. Use the word <u>accept</u> in a sentence.

_____

_____

5. Use the word <u>past</u> in a sentence.

_____

_____

Final Writing Assignment
Many colleges have spent millions of dollars on wiring for "smart" classrooms such as Internet-connected lecture halls in the belief that technology will transform the way we learn. Some professors plan to change the way they teach their courses. For example, students can view film clips, hear speeches, and rearrange the material, write about it, and share it with someone in another location. If you have had an opportunity to access the Internet, do you agree or disagree with using this method to teach college courses? Give specific examples of how a student can benefit from the access to the Internet. If you disagree with using the Internet to teach courses, give specific reasons for your opinions.

OR

Alternative Writing Assignment
How would conducting business in another culture differ from doing business in the American culture? For example, in a Japanese business meeting, if you try to deviate from the prearranged agenda and force consideration of a new topic, you might make the business people very uncomfortable. The emphasis on conformity in the Japanese culture discourages individual initiative. Further, when Westerners speak, the Japanese will often say, "Hai" (yes). A misunderstanding may arise because this hai means, "Yes, I understand you," not "Yes, I agree with you," as the American may assume.

If you are familiar with a different culture, explain how that culture's attitudes, speech patterns, and interpersonal behavior patterns would affect the way business is conducted. Compare and contrast those interactions with those in the United States.

TEST ANSWER KEY

Chapter Tests

Chapter 1, Form A
I. 1. O 2. N 3. N 4. O 5. O 6. N 7. O 8. O 9. N 10. N

II. 1. Gina, change, meter
2. Jim, Celtics, Boston Garden, Friday
3. Sofi, countries, Europe
4. Mr. Palka, dream, reality
5. Trash, streets, strike

III. 1. children's 2. year's 3. first-graders' 4. dentist's 5. Julius' (or Julius's)

IV. 1. speaker's notes 2. customers' compliments 3. father-in-law's career 4. family's plans
5. women's athletic club

V. 1. <u>them</u>--him or her (or change customer to customers)
2. <u>you</u>--we
3. <u>you</u>--them
4. <u>They</u>--he or she (or change to plural: motorists run)
5. <u>they</u>---he or she (or change to plural: people want)

VI. 1. its 2. your 3. theirs 4. ours 5. Whose

VII. Answers will vary.

VIII. 1. heroes 2. foxes 3. witches 4. mice 5. bounties

IX. 1. I 2. themselves 3. himself 4. ourselves 5. C

Chapter 1, Form B
I. 1. N 2. N 3. O 4. O 5. N 6. N 7. O 8. O 9. N 10. O

II. 1. disaster, courage, volunteers
2. sister, drugstore, summer
3. students, Lisa, job
4. driver, trunk, tire
5. Mr. Evans, notice, door

III. 1. governor's
2. mother's
3. Mr. Smith's
4. coach's
5. woman's

IV. 1. the two babies' eyes
2. Mrs. Marcus' (or Marcus's) husband

3. Marian's parents
4. three weeks' delay
5. the men's jackets

V. 1. <u>You</u>--she (verb should add an s)
2. <u>it</u>--they
3. <u>them</u>--him or her (or change customer is to customers are)
4. <u>you</u>--he
5. <u>they</u>--he or she (or change to people own boats)

VI. 1. its 2. Whose 3. your 4. ours 5. theirs

VII. Answers will vary.

VIII. 1. losses
2. wives
3. leaves
4. vetoes
5. parties

IX. 1. C 2. me 3. themselves 4. C 5. ourselves

Chapter 1, Form C
I. 1. N 2. N 3. O 4. N 5. N 6. O 7. O 8. N 9. N 10. O

II. 1. Firefighters, hours, break
2. children, basketball, Garrison Recreational Center
3. Khalida, ideas, journal
4. Drivers, coins, meter
5. roommate, lamp, sale

III. 1. sister-in-law's
2. story's
3. doctors'
4. Karen's
5. pilots'

IV. 1. Mrs. Sanchez's home
2. students' journals
3. boss's computer
4. men's hats
5. brother-in-law's name

V. 1. <u>they</u>—it
2. <u>them</u>—him or her
3. <u>you</u>—I
4. <u>your</u>—their
5. <u>them</u>—him or her

VI. 1. Whose 2. its 3. theirs 4. your 5. ours

VII. Sentences will vary.

VIII. 1. watches 2. bosses 3. paths 4. cash 5. duties

IX. 1. C 2. I 3. himself 4. ourselves 5. C

Chapter 2, Form A

I. 1. liked 2. rode 3. bought 4. was 5. looked

II. 1. could remember 2. were arguing 3. listened 4. Have visited 5. are
6. will give 7. had been 8. has made 9. vetoed 10. must have lost

III. 1. has or had 2. is or was 3. will 4. Are 5. has or had

IV. 1. will win 2. will drive 3. would understand 4. will play 5. will have

V. 1. had broken 2. will have fixed 3. had eaten 4. have gone 5. has taught

VI. 1. chooses	chose	chosen	choosing
2. supposes	supposed	supposed	supposing
3. carries	carried	carried	carrying
4. drinks	drank	drunk	drinking
5. is	was, were	been	being

VII. 1. Do [still] live 2. has [just] been closed 3. were [further] complicated 4. has [almost] finished 5.Has[n't] [already] made

Chapter 2, Form B

I. 1. taught 2. explained 3. slid 4. traveled 5. was

II. 1. is ending
2. had bought
3. has recorded
4. saw
5. have been standing
6. Did see
7. is making
8. had won
9. May borrow
10. worries

III. 1. has 2. has 3. is or was 4. has 5. has or had

IV. 1. will compete 2. will begin 3. would drive 4. will win 5. would be

V. 1. has or had made 2. had arrived 3. will have attended 4. had forgotten 5. has been

VI.

1. is,	was, were	been	being
2. writes	wrote	written	writing
3. puts	put	put	putting
4. loses	lost	lost	losing
5. replies	replied	replied	replying

VII. 1. has [just] given
2. has [never] been
3. Has[n't] [ever] ridden
4. is [actually] riding
5. did[n't] [even] cry

Chapter 2, Form C

I. 1. washed 2. sent 3. turned 4. sold 5. gave

II. 1. must be
2. Does suit
3. is
4. are riding
5. Should order
6. can prepare
7. may have left
8. Should take
9. has been
10. is talking

III. 1. is or was 2. has 3. Have 4. are or were 5. will

IV. 1. will forgive 2. will train 3. will wilt 4. would choose 5. would study

V. 1. had auditioned 2. will have traveled 3. have tried 4. has brought 5. has seen

VI.

1. has	had	had	having
2. buys	bought	bought	buying
3. hurries	hurried	hurried	hurrying
4. is,	was, were	been	being
5. brings	brought	brought	bringing

VII. 1. has [often] talked
2. Would[n't][rather] stay
3. is [usually] waiting
4. can [sometimes] be
5. are [n't] returning

Chapter 3, Form A

I. Subject	Aux. Verb	Main Verb
1. (You)		check
2. building		has
3. Who	will	win
4. Many	are	selling
5. car	does	have
6. packages	Did	arrive
7. aunt	has	visited
8. She		traveled
9. fire	must have	started
10. Joanne		moved

II. Prep. Phrase	Verb	Object of Verb
1. [in the last set]	played	solo
2. [from Florida]	has arrived	_____
3. [alongside the theater]	form	line
4. [for takeoff]	prepared	_____
5. [about a…experience]	wrote	essay

III. Answers may vary.

IV. Individual sentences may vary.

V. 1. I 2. her 3. him 4. me 5. she

VI. 1. [in the middle of the bridge] [for a long time]
2. [of us] [because of the traffic jam]
3. [through the dark] [despite the…rain]
4. [After the storm] [on the bridge]
5. [on account of the delay] [of the drivers]

VII. a. 1. He's 2. They're 3. She'll 4. It's 5. There's

b. Subject	Aux. Verb	Main Verb
1. He	is	leaving
2. They	are	going
3. She	will	drive
4. It		is
5. suitcase		is

Chapter 3, Form B

I. Subject	Aux. Verb	Main Verb
1. I	can	hear
2. (You)		come
3. Mr. Danner	is	leading
4. Renata	has	marched
5. We	have been	decorating

6. drum major	has		dropped
7. One	has		picked up
8. clown	will		twirl
9. crowd			laughs and applauds
10. you	do		love

II. Prep. Phrase	Verb	Object of Verb
1. [for an hour]	has been talking	_____
2. [around the auditorium] [at his friends]	looks	_____
3. [of poetry]	is reading	book
4. [during this lecture]	is taking	notes
5. no prepositional phrase	will finish	speech

III. Answers will vary.

IV. Answers will vary.

V. 1. I 2. him 3. she 4. I 5. him

VI. 1. [at the book store] [about the slow service]
2. [at the end] [of our block]
3. [In spite of his injured arm] [in the game]
4. [to the gym] [with Dwight]
5. [of the questions] [for me]

VII. a. 1. It's 2. She's 3. They'll 4. We're 5. You're

b. Subject	Auxiliary Verb	Main Verb
1. It		is
2. She	is	speaking
3. They	will	answer
4. We	are	leaving
5. You		are

Chapter 3, Form C

I. Subject	Aux. Verb	Main Verb
1. Mr. Arana	does	like
2. (You)		send
3. Pam	is	enjoying
4. I	can	read
5. you	would	lend
6. Ava ,Vic		work
7. café	has	opened
8. piano	should be	tuned
9. class		has
10. bookstore	will	have

II. Prepositional Phrase	Verb	Object of Verb

1.	[on the calendar]	marked	date
2.		do forget	it
3.		will visit	Akira
4.	[with me]	is staying	no object
5.	[from Texas][to Illinois] [on our trip] will drive		no object

III. Answers will vary.

IV. Sentences will vary.

V. 1. she 2. I 3.her 4. me 5. him, me

VI. 1. [in the Navy] [aboard the U.S.S. Cole]
2. [at sea] [for three months]
3. [of duty] [to the Middle East]
4. [from Turkey] [to the port] [in Yemen]
5. [throughout the voyage] [with her family]

VII. a. 1. I've 2. they'll 3. wasn't 4. you're 5. Jack's

b. Subject	Aux. Verb	Main Verb
1. I	have	invited
2. They	will	arrive
3. Jack		was
4. You	are	going
5. Jack	is	planning

Chapter 4, Form A
I. 1. [Some] [test][easier]
2. [warm] [sunny] [our]
3. [Mrs. Yasuda's] [accounting] [this]
4. [The] [gas] [full]
5. [That] [potato] [salty]

II. 1. fluently 2. seldom 3. ever 4. too 5. yesterday

III. 1. most (or least) understanding 2. fewer 3. most (or least) curious 4. most (or least) amazing
5. better

IV. 1. most or least emphatically 2. farther 3. best 4. more slowly 5. more carefully

V. 1. On the evening news, we watched the tornado destroy everything in its path.
2. Mrs. Scott tried to remove the spot in the carpeting with a strong detergent.
3. Through her office window, Mia watched the band marching in the parade.

VI. 1. After working overtime for several months I welcomed a vacation.
2. While Leon was repairing his fence, he smashed his finger with the hammer.
3. Harley was impressed by the salesman's words, so the motorcycle…

Chapter 4, Form B

I. 1. [My] [torn] [cowboy]
2. [That] [woman's] [bright]
3. [Every] [his] [new]
4. [two] [street] [a]
5. [Those] [three] [young]

II. 1. carefully 2. yesterday 3. never 4. sometimes 5. quickly

III. 1. easier 2. worst 3. most successful, or least successful 4. better 5. poorest

IV. 1. better 2. worse 3. more quickly, or less quickly 4. fastest
5. more often, or less often

V. 1. The driver had to leave his car with a flat tire by the side of the road.
2. Ardeth liked the view of the mountain from the window.
3. Ruth ate nearly a pound of grapes by herself.

VI. 1. If you sit too long in the sun, your skin can get sunburned.
2. When I was ten, my family traveled to Canada.
3. When Arnold was driving on Main Street, the traffic seemed heavy.

Chapter 4, Form C

I. 1. [his] [green] [blue]
2. [Some] [office] [express]
3. [Their] [a] [tile]
4. [This] [worn] [frayed]
5. [Deanna's] [an] [expensive]

II. 1. often 2. never 3. today 4. usually 5. hard

III. 1. most unusual 2. better 3. most isolated 4. more comfortable 5. softest

IV. 1. sooner 2. more clearly 3. higher 4. less efficiently 5. fastest

V. 1. Mei listened expectantly for the telephone to ring.
2. Ari ordered a sundae with whipped cream and nuts to go.
3. Roz walked by with her collie while we were washing the car.

VI. 1. When we were visiting the zoo nursery, the young attendants were feeding the baby gorillas.
2. When I was only a small child, my father bought me my first baseball glove.
3. While I was listening to the radio, the weatherman said that it would rain tomorrow.

Chapter 5, Form A

I. 1. MC
2. P
3. P
4. MC
5. MC

II. 1. Simple
2. Simple
3. Simple
4. Compound
5. Compound

III. 1. C streets; otherwise,
2. S Shalonda, indeed,
3. S rented, in fact,
4. C garage; however,
5. C lunch; instead,

IV. Answers will vary.
1. The world's largest skateboard park, which opened recently in Canada, has three separate areas: Intro Park, Central Park, and Expert Park.
2. Before the new public skate parks were built, skateboarders often damaged public property jumping from park benches or jumping over street curbs.
3. Cypress High School allows students not only to bring their skateboards to school, but also for using them as transportation to and from school.
4. This California high school plans to install sixty skateboard racks and to charge the students ten dollars per year for their use.
5. Skateboarding's most famous athlete has become a millionaire by competing, owning his own skate company, and marketing his own popular video games.

V. 1. <u>RO</u>…motel, and then next morning we were back on the road by 6 A.M.
2. <u>CS</u>…lunch; it will be served promptly after the meeting.
3. <u>RO</u> …masks, but he plans to donate them to a museum.
4. <u>CS</u> …neighborhood; however, many buyers are remodeling older homes.
5. <u>RO</u> …computer. Fortunately, the warranty covered the cost.

Chapter 5, Form B

I. 1. P
2. MC
3. P
4. MC
5. MC

II. 1. Compound
2. Compound
3. Simple

4. Simple
5. Compound

II. 1. C environment; nevertheless, few are willing to make the necessary personal sacrifices.
2. C governor; however, he didn't actually expect an answer.
3. S surprised, therefore, to receive a letter from her regarding the environment.
4. S governor, furthermore, invited him to visit the state capital during spring break.
5. C The plane was two hours late; consequently, Lyle nearly missed his connecting flight.

IV. Answers will vary.
1. The Italian immigrant Simon Rodia constructed Watts Towers on a dead-end street, near railroad tracks, on a triangular lot.
2. Rodia not only built this 992-foot sculpture by himself at night but also worked as a plasterer and tile setter during the day.
3. The spires of this folk-art masterpiece in Los Angeles were erected without the aid of machines, scaffolding, bolts, or rivets.
4. The artist had to reinforce his structure with discarded steel rods and pipes and even used bed frames and other castoffs.
5. Visitors especially admire the decorative broken glass, sea shells, and ceramic tiles on the towers.

V. 1. RO block, so a police officer gave me a ticket for jaywalking.
2. CS June; however, she….
3. CS minutes; he finally found a parking place.
4. CS times, but no one answered.
5. RO day; nevertheless, she voted (or however, as a result) .
Other connectives may be correct.

Chapter 5, Form C

I. 1. P
2. MC
3. MC
4. P
5. MC

II. 1. Compound
2. Compound
3. Simple
4. Simple
5. Simple

III. 1. C cut ;therefore,
2. S President, however, lacked
3. C delicious; however,
4. S wondered, moreover,
5. C film; nevertheless,

IV. Answers will vary.
1. The Akashi Kaikyo Bridge in Japan is the largest, tallest, and most expensive suspension bridge in the world.
2. In designing the Akashi Bridge, engineers knew that taking the extreme weather into account was as important as not blocking shipping traffic.
3. One of the four artificial islands on the Chesapeake Bay Bridge-Tunnel in Virginia offers drivers a parking lot, restrooms, a gift shop, and a scenic view.
4. Before the New River Gorge Bridge was built, travelers crossed the West Virginia gorge by making a 40-mile detour or by driving down narrow mountain roads.
5. Now drivers not only reduce their driving time to a minute, but also enjoy a beautiful view of the gorge.

V. 1. RO noon; however or nevertheless, we will
2. RO animal; they must
3. CS violence, so or and I have
4. RO Capistrano; however, they
5. CS stopped, but the instructor

Chapter 6, Form A

I. 1. [that]she must move soon.
2. [Although] Mrs. Turner likes New Jersey,
3. [because] her employer has opened a new office in Miami.
4. [while] they are living in Miami
5. [until] they buy one in Florida.

II. a. and b. Answers will vary.

III. Answers will vary.

IV. (Suggested sentences)
1. RO When Julia's children visit the park, they love…train.
2. CS …Terrell went to the YMCA where he learned to swim.
3. RO While Robin enjoys…city, Seth enjoys…country.
4. RO Last night, after Jamal returned from the meeting, he read the newspaper before dinner.
5. CS Garth is transferring to the Art Center because he …graphic artist.

V. a.	1. F	2. S	3. S	4. F	5. S
	6. F	7. S	8. F	9. S	10. S
	11. F	12. S			

V. b. Answers may vary, but these are possible answers.
1. Ever since …years old, she has wanted …broadcaster.
2. She has enrolled in college to prepare …career.
3. So far she …courses: Speech 1,…Beginning Broadcasting
4. While appearing …shows, she has met several famous people.
5. One of them …newscaster who has given her…break.

Chapter 6, Form B

I. 1. [that] Becky has rented is near the campus.
2. [Since] she lives so close to the campus, she walks to her classes.
3. [when] Leola moves in, she will share expenses with Becky.
4. [how] he could improve his grades in algebra.
5. [who] are tutors in the mathematics department.

II. a. and b. Answers will vary.

III. Answers will vary.

IV. (Suggested sentences)
1. CS   The two…game while their mother…lunch.
2. RO   Their oldest sister, who had a book review assigned for Monday, was reading.
3. CS   After Corey and Lamar had finished working, they … movie.
5. RO   We checked out a video from the library before we returned home.
6. CS   Although we had both seen the film before, we watched it to the end.

V. a.1. S   2. F   3. S   4. F   5. S
    6. S   7. F   8. S   9. F   10. S
    11. S   12. F

V. b. Answers may vary, but these are possible answers:
1. In my job at a bank, I … line.
2. Although they rarely answer me, I … morning."
3. I watch them scowl as they fill out the deposit slips.
4. Sometimes they mutter to themselves while they try to add the numbers.
5. They all look relieved and happy when they leave the bank.

Chapter 6, Form C

I. 1. [while] he is trying to study
2. [that] you found
3. [After] the farmer had bought the new truck
4. [who] had dance training
5. [until] everyone has been seated

II. a. and b. Answers will vary.

III. Answers will vary.

IV. Suggested sentences:
1. RO   Kevin hasn't saved enough money for tuition even though he…
2. CS   When Laura is on vacation, she likes to read….
3. RO   Since Mike entered college in the fall, he has had less….
4. CS   The film that won four awards is playing…Center.
5. CS   The football…as the band began to play.

V. a. 1.S   2. F   3. S   4. S   5. F
  6. F   7. F   8. S   9. S   10. F
  11. S   12. F

V. b. Answers may vary, but these are possible answers.
1. Now that the Limpopo River has receded considerably, plans are to rebuild on higher ground.
2. The elevated highway was overtaken by the raging river, requiring two boat journeys and about a fifty-minute walk between breaks.
3. The area is a wide, flat expanse, exposed to the ocean wind.
4. The powerful action of the river removed huge sections of asphalt pavement, lifted whole like ribbons of taffy and gently relocated downstream.
5. Still potent was the smell of a few cattle carcasses, which had been left to rot along the banks of the river.

Chapter 7, Form A

I. 1. has 2. increase 3. are 4. contributes 5. use

II. 1. apply 2. is 3. was 4. have 5. works

III. 1. her 2. its 3. he 4. its 5. his

IV. Answers may vary, but here are some possible sentences.
1. Many violent crimes have been committed in large cities.
2. When the police officer stopped the traffic, he enabled the ambulance….
3. After Dennis talked to a helicopter pilot, he knew that he wanted a job as a pilot.
4. The exciting final minutes of the game made the crowd roar.
5. Lynnette told Kim that Kim's paintings were beautiful.

V. Answers will vary.

Chapter 7, Form B

I. 1. have 2. appears 3. make 4. are 5. are

II. 1. is 2. has 3. were 4. likes 5. are

III. 1. their 2. her 3. its 4. its 5. her

IV. Answers may differ from these suggested answers.
1. Wally and Burt discussed their plans for the future. OR Wally and Burt discussed Wally's (or Burt's) plans for the future.
2. When Hank charged into a defensive player, the referee called a foul.
3. Annette has seen the same movie ten times this month. Seeing the movie ten times in one month is a new world's record.
4. When one lane of the freeway was closed for repairs, the traffic was slow-moving.
5. When the landlords raised the rents, the tenants complained.

V. Answers will vary.

Chapter 7, Form C

I. 1. are 2. were 3. describe 4. were 5. look

II. 1. has 2. shows 3. issues 4. is 5. argues

III. 1. their 2. her 3. his 4. its 5. their

IV. Answers may vary, but here are some possible sentences.
1. Tutoring is a rewarding occupation.
2. Their dog makes drivers nervous when it chases cars down the street.
3. Kevin told Alberto that Harrison would meet Alberto at the soccer field. or Kevin told Alberto, "Harrison will meet you at the soccer field."
4. Chinese food can be delicious.
5. Alan worked overtime for a month in order to buy a new leather jacket. or Because Alan wanted a new leather jacket, he had to work overtime for a month.

V. Sentences will vary.

Chapter 8, Form A.

I. 1. …the conditions, they still had to pick the crops.
2. Delores Ramirez, who…district, has a record of supporting farm legislation.
3. protesters, but they could not arrive at a settlement.
4. Three well-trained, young lawyers met with the workers.
5. No commas
6. Jonathan, when …the lawyer asked his partner.
7. … airport, Jonathan…hear a word his wife was saying.
8. …the torn, dirty, faded blue jeans.
9. …Cabot and Lodge, 2400 Beacon Street, Boston, Massachusetts.
10. … problems, and …progress had been made.
11. …post office, a bookstore, a supermarket, a Laundromat, and a pharmacy…of her new apartment.
12. … in, she enrolled in the local community college.
13. …September 14, 2005, and ended on January 22, 2006.
14. …learn, moreover, …child-care center.
15. … job, so she…center.
16. The Hillside Pharmacy, which was located on the corner of Prospect Avenue, …for new employees.
17. To reach the pharmacy, she had to walk only four blocks.
18. No commas
19. …time, but …to succeed.
20. …big, juicy hamburger and some crisp, golden French fries.

II. Answers will vary.

Chapter 8, Form B

I. 1. … jerseys, shorts, knee pads, and mouth guards…session.
2. … gym, turn left at the water fountain.
3. "Wait a minute, Alex," the cheerleader called, "and I'll go with you."
4. … March 13, but …for the trophy.
5. No commas
6. ... celebration, of course.
7. No commas
8. ... hungry, muscular basketball players.
9. …sandwich, and …for dessert.
10. party, they …was all gone.
11. …Adams, whose…photographer,…with him.
12. "I never know," he says, "when…my way."
13. …playoff, indeed, gave…opportunity.
14. No commas
15. …moment, and…peak of action.
16. Los Angeles Post, 2565 State Street, Los Angeles, California 91074, as…competition.
17. …category, but, best of all, it…Sunday paper.
18. To win this prize, Eliot…photographers.
19. On the following Monday, he…yellow pages.
20. … mat board, a mat cutter, aluminum framing, a piece of precut glass, and…photograph.

II. Answers will vary.

Chapter 8, Form C

I. 1. No commas
2. …books, several pens, a notebook, and a calculator.
3. No commas
4. "Denise,…discs," Marcus said, "…tomorrow night."
5. …President, the White House, Washington, D.C. 20500.
6. …afternoon, so…in the morning.
7. No commas
8. …work, as a rule, until noon.
9. On June 17, 2004, our son graduated from college.
10. …Office, but…one yet.
11. … carefully, Mario…assembled the bicycle.
12. No commas
13. …continued, nevertheless, to the finish line.
14. …Edison, who was…inventor,…Menlo Park.
15. …pool, she felt refreshed.
16. No commas
17. …enthusiastic, loyal…end of the game.
18. …months, Ben…every day.
19. Mt. McKinley, which…America, is 20,320 feet high.
20. …tough, hard-driving rookie cop in the film.

II. Answers will vary.

Chapter 9, Form A

I. 1. Mr. Jackson…waiting.
2. "He was safe by a mile!" … u¡ ire.
3. …11:15 A. M. and …2:12 P.N
4. Dr. Tan received his D. D. S. ¡   ee from USC ten years ago.
5.   … you?"… asked.

II. 1. … puzzled; the results…cε. ...ıly unexpected.
2. …dates: … friend's wedding.
3. toll-free number; she wanted…ten-speed bicycles.
4. …magazines: Time…Sports Illustrated.
5. …injury; however, many drivers refuse to buckle up.

III. 1. Last …Cancun, Mexico.
2. The….Sunday…June…Father's Day.
3. Captain Hardesty…Larchmont Community College.
4. Can… Mt. Rushmore?
5. Bing …Thompson …picnic food.

IV. 1. three Mts. $79.50
2. first A. M. Sept.
3. Five-hundred Ave. St.
4. Sen. C. W. Virginia
5. Ms. 62 86

V. Answers will vary.

Chapter 9, Form B

I. 1. Ms. Cheryl Kam.
2. Dr. Barnes's…9 A.M…5 P.M.
3. …job.
4. …again!
5. …basket?" he asked.

II. 1. . . .duties: shelving. . .circulation desk.
2. ...month; however, he…for him.
3. …surprised; the magazine…for publication.
4. …company; therefore,…he travels …countries.
5.   class: four pencils…a chamois cloth.

III.1. Delores…Sundays…Wednesdays off.
2.   Granny Smith…New Zealand's exports.
3.   I…I…Spanish and English.
4.   Valerie…Martin Luther King High School
5.   In August…Lake Louise.

125

IV. 1. third 21 to 20 USC
2.   Bros. two 7-percent
3.   Mrs. N. Korea Wall Street Journal
4.   Prof. twenty-two ten
5.   Jr. Ga. Jan.

V. Answers will vary.

Chapter 9, Form C

I. 1. …weigh.
2. …coffee?"… asked.
3. … A. A…June.
4. … truck!"…cried.
5. … D. C. next spring.

II. 1. …items: potatoes,…milk.
2. …Marathon; therefore, she…day.
3. … tomorrow; he…dash.
4. …points: the …clearly.
5. …car; repairing…expensive.

III.. 1. Annika …Lake Superior …summer.
2. …Italian citizen, Francesca … Southern California.
3. While …San Francisco, Jalena …Golden Gate Bridge.
4. Terrell rented a Ford Explorer from Mac's Car Rental.
5. On July 4th I usually take the Long Island Railroad to Jones Beach.

IV. 1. Capt. Ft. Wash.
2. 2 biographies 4 travel 12 novels
3. P.M. Mr. three
4. Gov. Asst. U.S.
5. $387.00 Co. $25.00

V. Answers will vary.

Midterm Exam
I. 1. gorillas'
2. women's
3. yours
4. Jennifer's
5. father's

II. 1. would finish
2. has brought
3. will forget
4. swam
5. had given

III.

Subject	Aux. Verb	Main Verb
1. we	should	see
2. William	has been	chosen
3. (You)		Turn
4. Ashley		was
5. All	must	make

IV. a. 1. The breeze felt cool to Brenda, skating through the park on a warm day.

2. Sue works after school for her brother who is a lawyer.

IV. b. Answers may vary, but here are some possible answers.

1. A magazine published John's first short story when he was sixteen.

2. After Jamal had run around the track three times, a cool drink tasted delicious.

3. Having served in World War I, Hemingway wrote a *Farewell to Arms* about his Italian army experiences.

Final Exam

I. a. 1. someone's

2. Adams' or Adam's

3. Today's

4. club's

5. Men's

I. b. 1. would stop

2. had fallen

3. chose

4. will have repaired

5. has spoken

II. a. 1. ...rice in small covered containers.

2. ...baskets nearly every Saturday afternoon with his neighbor, Kirby.

b. 1. Allen dropped the ball, making his second error of the game.

2. After leaving the bank, Calvin discovered that his ATM card was missing.

3. A budget seemed the best way to start saving money for my vacation. or
As I was determined...

III. 1. ...her serve; therefore,...this semester.

2. ...over-exposed; others were perfect.

3. ...class time, but...

4. ...floor while I washed ...

5. ... cancer; nevertheless, ...to smoke.

IV. 1. I 2. need 3. its 4. is 5. have

V. 1. ...performs, Bradley...concerts.

2. ...3356 Kern Avenue, Canton, Ohio.

3. ...bread crumbs, tomato sauce, onions, and ground beef.

4. ...September 3, 1998, John and Marie were married.

5. …Jackson, who...paper, …journalist.

VI. 1. While Ben... breakfast, he…newspaper.
2. During... Secretary of State... countries: France, Germany, Japan, and Poland.
3. Toby... Senator Mark Russell at 2:30 P.M. today.
4. I…Spanish…semester.
5. Taylor... Whitney Houston ...*Ebony.*

VII. Answers will vary.